SHEPHERD OF HERMAS

COLLECTION

2 BOOKS

AETERNA PRESS

PUBLISHED BY AETERNA PRESS.
COVER DESIGN BY AETERNA PRESS.

ISBN-13: 978-1-78647-113-0

AVAILABLE AS AN E-BOOK:
WWW.AETERNAPRESS.COM

CONTENTS

SHEPHERD OF HERMAS COLLECTION

The Shepherd of Hermas is a Christian literary work of the late 1st or mid-2nd century, considered a valuable book by many Christians, and considered canonical scripture by some of the early Church fathers such as Irenaeus. The Shepherd was very popular amongst Christians in the 2nd and 3rd centuries. It was bound as part of the New Testament in the Codex Sinaiticus, and it was listed between the Acts of the Apostles and the Acts of Paul in the stichometrical list of the Codex Claromontanus. The work comprises five visions, twelve mandates, and ten parables. It relies on allegory and pays special attention to the Church, calling the faithful to repent of the sins that have harmed it.

THE PASTOR OF HERMAS

HERMAS

AVAILABLE IN PAPERBACK.

TRANSLATED BY THE REV. F. CROMBIE, M.A.

ANF02. FATHERS OF THE SECOND CENTURY: HERMAS, TATIAN, ATHENAGORAS, THEOPHILUS, AND CLEMENT OF ALEXANDRIA (ENTIRE). SCHAFF, PHILIP (1819–1893) EDITOR.

THE PASTOR OF HERMAS

Book First

Visions

VISION FIRST

AGAINST FILTHY AND PROUD THOUGHTS, AND THE CARELESSNESS OF HERMAS IN CHASTISING HIS SONS

CHAP. I

He who had brought me up, sold me to one Rhode in Rome. Many years after this I recognised her, and I began to love her as a sister. Some time after, I saw her bathe in the river Tiber; and I gave her my hand, and drew her out of the river. The sight of her beauty made me think with myself, "I should be a happy man if I could but get a wife as handsome and good as she is." This was the only thought that passed through me: this and nothing more. A short time after this, as I was walking on my road to the villages, and magnifying the creatures of God, and thinking how magnificent, and beautiful, and powerful they are, I fell asleep. And the Spirit carried me away, and took me through a pathless place, through which a man could not travel, for it was situated in the midst of rocks; it was rugged and impassible on account of water. Having passed over this river, I came to a plain. I then bent down on my knees, and began to pray to the Lord, and to confess my sins. And as I prayed, the heavens were opened, and I see the woman whom I had desired saluting me from the sky, and saying, "Hail, Hermas!" And looking up to her, I said, "Lady, what doest thou here?" And she answered me, "I have been taken up here to accuse you of your sins before the Lord." "Lady," said I, "are you to be the subject of my accusation?" "No," said she; "but hear the words which I am going to speak to you. God, who dwells in the heavens, and made out of nothing the things that exist, and multiplied and increased them on account of His holy Church, is angry with you for having sinned against me." I answered her, "Lady, have I sinned against you? How? or when spoke I an unseemly word to you? Did I not always think of you as a lady? Did I not always respect you as a sister? Why do you falsely accuse me of this wickedness and impurity?" With a smile she replied to me, "The desire of wickedness arose within your heart. Is it not your opinion that a righteous man commits sin when an evil desire arises in his heart? There is sin in such a case, and the sin is great," said she; "for the thoughts of a righteous man should be righteous. For by thinking righteously his character is established in the heavens, and he has the Lord merciful to him in every business. But such as entertain wicked thoughts in their minds are bringing upon themselves death and captivity; and especially is this the case with those who set their affections on this world, and glory in their riches, and look not forward to the blessings of the life to come. For many will their regrets be; for they have no hope, but have despaired of themselves and their life. But do thou pray to God, and He will heal thy sins, and the sins of thy whole house, and of all the saints."

CHAP. II

After she had spoken these words, the heavens were shut. I was overwhelmed with sorrow and fear, and said to myself, "If this sin is assigned to me, how can I be saved, or how shall I propitiate God in regard to my sins, which are of the grossest character? With what words shall I ask the Lord to be merciful to me?" While I was thinking over these things, and discussing them in my mind, I saw opposite to me a chair, white, made of white wool, of great size. And there came up an old woman, arrayed in a splendid robe, and with a book in her hand; and she sat down alone, and saluted me, "Hail, Hermas!" And in sadness and tears I said to her, "Lady, hail!" And she said to me, "Why are you downcast, Hermas? for you were wont to be patient and temperate, and always smiling. Why are you so gloomy, and not cheerful?" I answered her and said, "O Lady, I have been reproached by a very good woman, who says that I sinned against her." And she said, "Far be such a deed from a servant of God. But perhaps a desire after her has arisen within your heart. Such a wish, in the case of the servants of God, produces sin. For it is a wicked and horrible wish in an all-chaste and already well-tried spirit to desire an evil deed; and especially for Hermas so to do, who keeps himself from all wicked desire, and is full of all simplicity, and of great guilelessness."

CHAP. III

"But God is not angry with you on account of this, but that you may convert your house, which have committed iniquity against the Lord, and against you, their parents. And although you love your sons, yet did you not warn your house, but permitted them to be terribly corrupted. On this account is the Lord angry with you, but He will heal all the evils which have been done in your house. For, on account of their sins and iniquities, you have been destroyed by the affairs of this world. But now the mercy of the Lord has taken pity on you and your house, and will strengthen you, and establish you in his glory. Only be not easy-minded, but be of good courage and comfort your house. For as a smith hammers out his work, and accomplishes whatever he wishes , so shall righteous daily speech overcome all iniquity. Cease not therefore to admonish your sons; for I know that, if they will repent with all their heart, they will be enrolled in the Books of Life with the saints." Having ended these words, she said to me, "Do you wish to hear me read?" I say to her, "Lady, I do." "Listen then, and give ear to the glories of God." And then I heard from her, magnificently and admirably, things which my memory could not retain. For all the words were terrible, such as man could not endure. The last words, however, I did remember; for they were useful to us, and gentle. "Lo, the God of powers, who by His invisible strong power and great wisdom has created the world, and by His glorious counsel has surrounded His creation with beauty, and by His strong word has fixed the heavens and laid the foundations of the earth upon the waters, and by His own wisdom and providence has created His holy Church, which He has blessed, lo! He removes the heavens and the mountains, the hills and the seas, and all things become plain to His elect, that He may bestow on them the blessing which He has promised them, with much glory and joy, if only they shall keep the commandments of God which they have received in great faith."

CHAP. IV

When she had ended her reading, she rose from the chair, and four young men came and carried off the chair and went away to the east. And she called me to herself and touched my breast, and said to me, "Have you been pleased with my reading?" And I say to her, "Lady, the last words please me, but the first are cruel and harsh." Then she said to me, "The last are for the righteous: the first are for heathens and apostates." And while she spoke to me, two men appeared and raised her on their shoulders, and they went to where the chair was in the east. With joyful countenance did she depart; and as she went, she said to me, "Behave like a man, Hermas."

VISION SECOND

AGAIN, OF HIS NEGLECT IN CHASTISING HIS TALKATIVE WIFE AND HIS LUSTFUL SONS, AND OF HIS CHARACTER

CHAP. I

As I was going to the country about the same time as on the previous year, in my walk I recalled to memory the vision of that year. And again the Spirit carried me away, and took me to the same place where I had been the year before. On coming to that place, I bowed my knees and began to pray to the Lord, and to glorify His name, because He had deemed me worthy, and had made known to me my former sins. On rising from prayer, I see opposite me that old woman, whom I had seen the year before, walking and reading some book. And she says to me, "Can you carry a report of these things to the elect of God?" I say to her, "Lady, so much I cannot retain in my memory, but give me the book and I shall transcribe it." "Take it," says she, "and you will give it back to me." Thereupon I took it, and going away into a certain part of the country, I transcribed the whole of it letter by letter; but the syllables of it I did not catch. No sooner, however, had I finished the writing of the book, than all of a sudden it was snatched from my hands; but who the person was that snatched it, I saw not.

CHAP. II

Fifteen days after, when I had fasted and prayed much to the Lord, the knowledge of the writing was revealed to me. Now the writing was to this effect: "Your seed, O Hermas, has sinned against God, and they have blasphemed against the Lord, and in their great wickedness they have betrayed their parents. And they passed as traitors of their parents, and by their treachery did they not reap profit. And even now they have added to their sins lusts and iniquitous pollutions, and thus their iniquities have been filled up. But make known these words to all your children, and to your wife, who is to be your sister. For she does not restrain her tongue, with which she commits iniquity; but, on hearing these words, she will control herself, and will obtain mercy. For after you have made known to them these words which my Lord has commanded me to reveal to you, then shall they be forgiven all the sins which in former times they committed, and forgiveness will be granted to all the saints who have sinned even to the present day, if they repent with all their heart, and drive all doubts from their minds. For the Lord has sworn by His glory, in regard to His elect, that if any one of them sin after a certain day which has been fixed, he shall not be saved. For the repentance of the righteous has limits. Filled up are the days of repentance to all the saints; but to the heathen, repentance will be possible even to the last day. You will tell, therefore, those who preside over the Church, to direct their ways in righteousness, that they may receive in full the promises with great glory. Stand stedfast, therefore, ye who work righteousness, and doubt not, that your passage may be with the holy angels. Happy ye who endure the great tribulation that is coming on, and happy they who shall not deny their own life. For the Lord hath sworn by His Son, that those who denied their Lord have abandoned their life in despair, for even now these are to deny Him in the days that are coming. To those who denied in earlier times, God became gracious, on account of His exceeding tender mercy."

CHAP. III

"But as for you, Hermas, remember not the wrongs done to you by your children, nor neglect your sister, that they may be cleansed from their former sins. For they will be instructed with righteous instruction, if you remember not the wrongs they have done you. For the remembrance of wrongs worketh death. And you, Hermas, have endured great personal tribulations on account of the transgressions of your house, because you did not attend to them, but were careless and engaged in your wicked transactions. But you are saved, because you did not depart from the living God, and on account of your simplicity and great self-control. These have saved you, if you remain stedfast. And they will save all who act in the same manner, and walk in guilelessness and simplicity. Those who possess such virtues will wax strong against every form of wickedness, and will abide unto eternal life. Blessed are all they who practice righteousness, for they shall never be destroyed. Now you will tell Maximus: Lo! tribulation cometh on. If it seemeth good to thee, deny again. The Lord is near to them who return unto Him, as it is written in Eldad and Modat, who prophesied to the people in the wilderness."

CHAP. IV

Now a revelation was given to me, my brethren, while I slept, by a young man of comely appearance, who said to me, "Who do you think that old woman is from whom you received the book?" And I said, "The Sibyl." "You are in a mistake," says he; "it is not the Sibyl." "Who is it then?" say I. And he said, "It is the Church." And I said to him, "Why then is she an old woman?" "Because," said he, "she was created first of all. On this account is she old. And for her sake was the world made." After that I saw a vision in my house, and that old woman came and asked me, if I had yet given the book to the presbyters. And I said that I had not. And then she said, "You have done well, for I have some words to add. But when I finish all the words, all the elect will then become acquainted with them through you. You will write therefore two books, and you will send the one to Clemens and the other to Grapte. And Clemens will send his to foreign countries, for permission has been granted to him to do so. And Grapte will admonish the widows and the orphans. But you will read the words in this city, along with the presbyters who preside over the Church."

VISION THIRD

CONCERNING THE BUILDING OF THE TRIUMPHANT CHURCH, AND THE VARIOUS CLASSES OF REPROBATE MEN

CHAP. I

The vision which I saw, my brethren, was of the following nature. Having fasted frequently, and having prayed to the Lord that He would show me the revelation which He promised to show me through that old woman, the same night that old woman appeared to me, and said to me, "Since you are so anxious and eager to know all things, go into the part of the country where you tarry; and about the fifth hour I shall appear unto you, and show you all that you ought to see." I asked her, saying "Lady, into what part of the country am I to go?" And she said, "Into any part you wish." Then I chose a spot which was suitable, and retired. Before, however, I began to speak and to mention the place, she said to me, "I will come where you wish." Accordingly, I went to the country, and counted the hours, and reached the place where I had promised to meet her. And I see an ivory seat ready placed, and on it a linen cushion, and above the linen cushion was spread a covering of fine linen. Seeing these laid out, and yet no one in the place, I began to feel awe, and as it were a trembling seized hold of me, and my hair stood on end, and as it were a horror came upon me when I saw that I was all alone. But on coming back to myself and calling to mind the glory of God, I took courage, bent my knees, and again confessed my sins to God as I had done before. Whereupon the old woman approached, accompanied by six young men whom I had also seen before; and she stood behind me, and listened to me, as I prayed and confessed my sins to the Lord. And touching me she said, "Hermas, cease praying continually for your sins; pray for righteousness, that you may have a portion of it immediately in your house." On this, she took me up by the hand, and brought me to the seat, and said to the young men, "Go and build." When the young men had gone and we were alone, she said to me, "Sit here." I say to her, "Lady, permit my elders to be seated first." "Do what I bid you," said she; "sit down." When I would have sat down on her right, she did not permit me, but with her hand beckoned to me to sit down on the left. While I was thinking about this, and feeling vexed that she did not let me sit on the right, she said, "Are you vexed, Hermas? The place to the right is for others who have already pleased God, and have suffered for His name's sake; and you have yet much to accomplish before you can sit with them. But abide as you now do in your simplicity, and you will sit with them, and with all who do their deeds and bear what they have borne."

CHAP. II

"What have they borne?" said I. "Listen," said she: "scourges, prisons, great tribulations, crosses, wild beasts, for God's name's sake. On this account is assigned to them the division of sanctification on the right hand, and to every one who shall suffer for God's name: to the rest is assigned the division on the left. But both for those who sit on the right, and those who sit on the left, there are the same gifts and promises; only those sit on the right, and have some glory. You then are eager to sit on the right with them, but your shortcomings are many. But you will be cleansed from your shortcomings; and all who are not given to doubts shall be cleansed from all their iniquities up till this day." Saying this, she wished to go away. But falling down at her feet, I begged her by the Lord that she would show me the vision which she had promised to show me. And then she again took hold of me by the hand, and raised me, and made me sit on the seat to the left; and lifting up a splendid rod, she said to me, "Do you see something great?" And I say, "Lady, I see nothing." She said to me, "Lo! do you not see opposite to you a great tower, built upon the waters, of splendid square stones?" For the tower was built square by those six young men who had come with her. But myriads of men were carrying stones to it, some dragging them from the depths, others removing them from the land, and they handed them to these six young men. They were taking them and building; and those of the stones that were dragged out of the depths, they placed in the building just as they were: for they were polished and fitted exactly into the other stones, and became so united one with another that the lines of juncture could not be perceived. And in this way the building of the tower looked as if it were made out of one stone. Those stones, however, which were taken from the earth suffered a different fate; for the young men rejected some of them, some they fitted into the building, and some they cut down, and cast far away from the tower. Many other stones, however, lay around the tower, and the young men did not use them in building; for some of them were rough, others had cracks in them, others had been made too short, and others were white and round, but did not fit into the building of the tower. Moreover, I saw other stones thrown far away from the tower, and falling into the public road; yet they did not remain on the road, but were rolled into a pathless place. And I saw others falling into the fire and burning, others falling close to the water, and yet not capable of being rolled into the water, though they wished to be rolled down, and to enter the water.

CHAP. III

On showing me these visions, she wished to retire. I said to her, "What is the use of my having seen all this, while I do not know what it means?" She said to me, "You are a cunning fellow, wishing to know everything that relates to the tower." "Even so, O Lady," said I, "that I may tell it to my brethren, that, hearing this, they may know the Lord in much glory." And she said, "Many indeed shall hear, and hearing, some shall be glad, and some shall weep. But even these, if they hear and repent, shall also rejoice. Hear, then, the parables of the tower; for I will reveal all to you, and give me no more trouble in regard to revelation: for these revelations have an end, for they have been completed. But you will not cease praying for revelations, for you are shameless. The tower which you see building is myself, the Church, who have appeared to you now and on the former occasion. Ask, then, whatever you like in regard to the tower, and I will reveal it to you, that you may rejoice with the saints." I said unto her, "Lady, since you have vouchsafed to reveal all to me this once, reveal it." She said to me, "Whatsoever ought to be revealed, will be revealed; only let your heart be with God, and doubt not whatsoever you shall see." I asked her, "Why was the tower built upon the waters, O Lady?" She answered, "I told you before, and you still inquire carefully: therefore inquiring you shall find the truth. Hear then why the tower is built upon the waters. It is because your life has been, and will be, saved through water. For the tower was founder on the word of the almighty and glorious Name and it is kept together by the invisible power of the Lord."

CHAP. IV

In reply I said to her, "This is magnificent and marvellous. But who are the six young men who are engaged in building?" And she said, "These are the holy angels of God, who were first created, and to whom the Lord handed over His whole creation, that they might increase and build up and rule over the whole creation. By these will the building of the tower be finished." "But who are the other persons who are engaged in carrying the stones?" "These also are holy angels of the Lord, but the former six are more excellent than these. The building of the tower will be finished, and all will rejoice together around the tower, and they will glorify God, because the tower is finished." I asked her, saying, "Lady, I should like to know what became of the stones, and what was meant by the various kinds of stones?" In reply she said to me, "Not because you are more deserving than all others that this revelation should be made to you—for there are others before you, and better than you, to whom these visions should have been revealed—but that the name of God may be glorified, has the revelation been made to you, and it will be made on account of the doubtful who ponder in their hearts whether these things will be or not. Tell them that all these things are true, and that none of them is beyond the truth. All of them are firm and sure, and established on a strong foundation."

CHAP. V

"Hear now with regard to the stones which are in the building. Those square white stones which fitted exactly into each other, are apostles, bishops, teachers, and deacons, who have lived in godly purity, and have acted as bishops and teachers and deacons chastely and reverently to the elect of God. Some of them have fallen asleep, and some still remain alive. And they have always agreed with each other, and been at peace among themselves, and listened to each other. On account of this, they join exactly into the building of the tower." "But who are the stones that were dragged from the depths, and which were laid into the building and fitted in with the rest of the stones previously placed in the tower?" "They are those who suffered for the Lord's sake." "But I wish to know, O Lady, who are the other stones which were carried from the land." "Those," she said, "which go into the building without being polished, are those whom God has approved of, for they walked in the straight ways of the Lord and practiced His commandments." "But who are those who are in the act of being brought and placed in the building?" "They are those who are young in faith and are faithful. But they are admonished by the angels to do good, for no iniquity has been found in them." "Who then are those whom they rejected and cast away?" "These are they who have sinned, and wish to repent. On this account they have not been thrown far from the tower, because they will yet be useful in the building, if they repent. Those then who are to repent, if they do repent, will be strong in faith, if they now repent while the tower is building. For if the building be finished, there will not be more room for any one, but he will be rejected. This privilege, however, will belong only to him who has now been placed near the tower."

CHAP. VI

"As to those who were cut down and thrown far away from the tower, do you wish to know who they are? They are the sons of iniquity, and they believed in hypocrisy, and wickedness did not depart from them. For this reason they are not saved, since they cannot be used in the building on account of their iniquities. Wherefore they have been cut off and cast far away on account of the anger of the Lord, for they have roused Him to anger. But I shall explain to you the other stones which you saw lying in great numbers, and not going into the building. Those which are rough are those who have known the truth and not remained in it, nor have they been joined to the saints. On this account are they unfit for use." "Who are those that have rents?" "These are they who are at discord in their hearts one with another, and are not at peace amongst themselves: they indeed keep peace before each other, but when they separate one from the other, their wicked thoughts remain in their hearts. These, then, are the rents which are in the stones. But those which are shortened are those who have indeed believed, and have the larger share of righteousness; yet they have also a considerable share of iniquity, and therefore they are shortened and not whole." "But who are these, Lady, that are white and round, and yet do not fit into the building of the tower?" She answered and said, "How long will you be foolish and stupid, and continue to put every kind of question and understand nothing? These are those who have faith indeed, but they have also the riches of this world. When, therefore, tribulation comes, on account of their riches and business they deny the Lord." I answered and said to her,

"When, then, will they be useful for the building, Lady?" "When the riches that now seduce them have been circumscribed, then will they be of use to God. For as a round stone cannot become square unless portions be cut off and cast away, so also those who are rich in this world cannot be useful to the Lord unless their riches be cut down. Learn this first from your own case. When you were rich, you were useless; but now you are useful and fit for life. Be ye useful to God; for you also will be used as one of these stones."

CHAP. VII

"Now the other stones which you saw cast far away from the tower, and falling upon the public road and rolling from it into pathless places, are those who have indeed believed, but through doubt have abandoned the true road. Thinking, then, that they could find a better, they wander and become wretched, and enter upon pathless places. But those which fell into the fire and were burned are those who have departed for ever from the living God; nor does the thought of repentance ever come into their hearts, on account of their devotion to their lusts and to the crimes which they committed. Do you wish to know who are the others which fell near the waters, but could not be rolled into them? These are they who have heard the word, and wish to be baptized in the name of the Lord; but when the chastity demanded by the truth comes into their recollection, they draw back, and again walk after their own wicked desires." She finished her exposition of the tower. But I, shameless as I yet was, asked her, "Is repentance possible for all those stones which have been cast away and did not fit into the building of the tower, and will they yet have a place in this tower?" "Repentance," said she, "is yet possible, but in this tower they cannot find a suitable place. But in another and much inferior place they will be laid, and that, too, only when they have been tortured and completed the days of their sins. And on this account will they be transferred, because they have partaken of the righteous Word. And then only will they be removed from their punishments when the thought of repenting of the evil deeds which they have done has come into their hearts. But if it does not come into their hearts, they will not be saved, on account of the hardness of their heart."

CHAP. VIII

When then I ceased asking in regard to all these matters, she said to me, "Do you wish to see anything else?" And as I was extremely eager to see something more, my countenance beamed with joy. She looked towards me with a smile, and said, "Do you see seven women around the tower?" "I do, Lady," said I. "This tower," said she, "is supported by them according to the precept of the Lord. Listen now to their functions. The first of them, who is clasping her hands, is called Faith. Through her the elect of God are saved. Another, who has her garments tucked up and acts with vigour, is called Self-restraint. She is the daughter of Faith. Whoever then follows her will become happy in his life, because he will restrain himself from all evil works, believing that, if he restrain himself from all evil desire, he will inherit eternal life." "But the others," said I, "O Lady, who are they?" And she said to me, "They are daughters of each other. One of them is called Simplicity, another Guilelessness, another Chastity, another Intelligence, another Love. When then you do all the works of their mother, you will be able to live." "I should like to know," said I, "O Lady, what power each one of them possesses." "Hear," she said, "what power they have. Their powers are regulated by each other, and follow each other in the order of their birth. For from Faith arises Self-restraint; from Self-restraint, Simplicity; from Simplicity, Guilelessness; from Guilelessness, Chastity; from Chastity, Intelligence; and from Intelligence, Love. The deeds, then, of these are pure, and chaste, and divine. Whoever devotes himself to these, and is able to hold fast by their works, shall have his dwelling in the tower with the saints of God." Then I asked her in regard to the ages, if now there is the conclusion. She cried out with a loud voice, "Foolish man! do you not see the tower yet building? When the tower is finished and built, then comes the end; and I assure you it will be soon finished. Ask me no more questions. Let you and all the saints be content with what I have called to your remembrance, and with my renewal of your spirits. But observe that it is not for your own sake only that these revelations have been made to you, but they have been given you that you may show them to all. For after three days—this you will take care to remember—I Command you to speak all the words which I am to say to you into the ears of the saints, that hearing them and doing them, they may be cleansed from their iniquities, and you along with them."

CHAP. IX

Give ear unto me, O Sons: I have brought you up in much simplicity, and guilelessness, and chastity, on account of the mercy of the Lord, who has dropped His righteousness down upon you, that ye may be made righteous and holy from all your iniquity and depravity; but you do not wish to rest from your iniquity. Now, therefore, listen to me, and be at peace one with another, and visit each other, and bear each other's burdens, and do not partake of God's creatures alone, but give abundantly of them to the needy. For some through the abundance of their food produce weakness in their flesh, and thus corrupt their flesh; while the flesh of others who have no food is corrupted, because they have not sufficient nourishment. And on this account their bodies waste away. This intemperance in eating is thus injurious to you who have abundance and do not distribute among those who are needy. Give heed to the judgment that is to come. Ye, therefore, who are high in position, seek out the hungry as long as the tower is not yet finished; for after the tower is finished, you will wish to do good, but will find no opportunity. Give heed, therefore, ye who glory in your wealth, lest those who are needy should groan, and their groans should ascend to the Lord, and ye be shut out with all your goods beyond the gate of the tower. Wherefore I now say to you who preside over the Church and love the first seats, "Be not like to drug-mixers. For the drug-mixers carry their drugs in boxes, but ye carry your drug and poison in your heart. Ye are hardened, and do not wish to cleanse your hearts, and to add unity of aim to purity of heart, that you may have mercy from the great King. Take heed, therefore, children, that these dissensions of yours do not deprive you of your life. How will you instruct the elect of the Lord, if you yourselves have not instruction? Instruct each other therefore, and be at peace among yourselves, that I also, standing joyful before your Father, may give an account of you all to your Lord."

CHAP. X

On her ceasing to speak to me, those six young men who were engaged in building came and conveyed her to the tower, and other four lifted up the seat and carried it also to the tower. The faces of these last I did not see, for they were turned away from me. And as she was going, I asked her to reveal to me the meaning of the three forms in which she appeared to me. In reply she said to me: "With regard to them, you must ask another to reveal their meaning to you." For she had appeared to me, brethren, in the first vision the previous year under the form of an exceedingly old woman, sitting in a chair. In the second vision her face was youthful, but her skin and hair betokened age, and she stood while she spoke to me. She was also more joyful than on the first occasion. But in the third vision she was entirely youthful and exquisitely beautiful, except only that she had the hair of an old woman; but her face beamed with joy, and she sat on a seat. Now I was exceeding sad in regard to these appearances, for I longed much to know what the visions meant. Then I see the old woman in a vision of the night saying unto me: "Every prayer should be accompanied with humility: fast, therefore, and you will obtain from the Lord what you beg." I fasted therefore for one day.

That very night there appeared to me a young man, who said, "Why do you frequently ask revelations in prayer? Take heed lest by asking many things you injure your flesh: be content with these revelations. Will you be able to see greater revelations than those which you have seen?" I answered and said to him, "Sir, one thing only I ask, that in regard to these three forms the revelation may be rendered complete." He answered me, "How long are ye senseless? But your doubts make you senseless, because you have not your hearts turned towards the Lord." But I answered and said to him, "From you, sir, we shall learn these things more accurately."

CHAP. XI

"Hear then," said he, "with regard to the three forms, concerning which you are inquiring. Why in the first vision did she appear to you as an old woman seated on a chair? Because your spirit is now old and withered up, and has lost its power in consequence of your infirmities and doubts. For, like elderly men who have no hope of renewing their strength, and expect nothing but their last sleep, so you, weakened by worldly occupations, have given yourselves up to sloth, and have not cast your cares upon the Lord. Your spirit therefore is broken, and you have grown old in your sorrows." "I should like then to know, sir, why she sat on a chair?" He answered, "Because every weak person sits on a chair on account of his weakness, that his weakness may be sustained. Lo! you have the form of the first vision."

CHAP. XII

"Now in the second vision you saw her standing with a youthful countenance, and more joyful than before; still she had the skin and hair of an aged woman. Hear," said he, "this parable also. When one becomes somewhat old, he despairs of himself on account of his weakness and poverty, and looks forward to nothing but the last day of his life. Then suddenly an inheritance is left him: and hearing of this, he rises up, and becoming exceeding joyful, he puts on strength. And now he no longer reclines, but stands up; and his spirit, already destroyed by his previous actions, is renewed, and he no longer sits, but acts with vigour. So happened it with you on hearing the revelation which God gave you. For the Lord had compassion on you, and renewed your spirit, and ye laid aside your infirmities. Vigour arose within you, and ye grew strong in faith; and the Lord, seeing your strength, rejoiced. On this account He showed you the building of the tower; and He will show you other things, if you continue at peace with each other with all your heart."

CHAP. XIII

"Now, in the third vision, you saw her still younger, and she was noble and joyful, and her shape was beautiful. For, just as when some good news comes suddenly to one who is sad, immediately he forgets his former sorrows, and looks for nothing else than the good news which he has heard, and for the future is made strong for good, and his spirit is renewed on account of the joy which he has received; so ye also have received the renewal of your spirits by seeing these good things. As to your seeing her sitting on a seat, that means that her position is one of strength, for a seat has four feet and stands firmly. For the world also is kept together by means of four elements. Those, therefore, who repent completely and with the whole heart, will become young and firmly established. You now have the revelation completely given you. Make no further demands for revelations. If anything ought to be revealed, it will be revealed to you."

VISION FOURTH

CONCERNING THE TRIAL AND TRIBULATION THAT ARE TO COME UPON MEN

CHAP. I

Twenty days after the former vision I saw another vision, brethren—a representation of the tribulation that is to come. I was going to a country house along the Campanian road. Now the house lay about ten furlongs from the public road. The district is one rarely traversed. And as I walked alone, I prayed the Lord to complete the revelations which He had made to me through His holy Church, that He might strengthen me, and give repentance to all His servants who were going astray, that His great and glorious name might be glorified because He vouchsafed to show me His marvels. And while I was glorifying Him and giving Him thanks, a voice, as it were, answered me, "Doubt not, Hermas;" and I began to think with myself, and to say, "What reason have I to doubt—I who have been established by the Lord, and who have seen such glorious sights?" I advanced a little, brethren, and, lo! I see dust rising even to the heavens. I began to say to myself, "Are cattle approaching and raising the dust?" It was about a furlong's distance from me. And, lo! I see the dust rising more and more, so that I imagined that it was something sent from God. But the sun now shone out a little, and, lo! I see a mighty beast like a whale, and out of its mouth fiery locusts proceeded. But the size of that beast was about a hundred feet, and it had a head like an urn. I began to weep, and to call on the Lord to rescue me from it. Then I remembered the word which I had heard, "Doubt not, O Hermas." Clothed, therefore, my brethren, with faith in the Lord and remembering the great things which He had taught me, I boldly faced the beast. Now that beast came on with such noise and force, that it could itself have destroyed a city. I came near it, and the monstrous beast stretched itself out on the ground, and showed nothing but its tongue, and did not stir at all until I had passed by it. Now the beast had four colours on its head—black, then fiery and bloody, then golden, and lastly white.

CHAP. II

Now after I had passed by the wild beast, and had moved forward about thirty feet, lo! a virgin meets me, adorned as if she were proceeding from the bridal chamber, clothed entirely in white, and with white sandals, and veiled up to her forehead, and her head was covered by a hood. And she had white hair. I knew from my former visions that this was the Church, and I became more joyful. She saluted me, and said, "Hail, O man!" And I returned her salutation, and said, "Lady, hail!" And she answered, and said to me, "Has nothing crossed your path?" I say, "I was met by a beast of such a size that it could destroy peoples, but through the power of the Lord and His great mercy I escaped from it." "Well did you escape from it," says she, "because you cast your care on God, and opened your heart to the Lord, believing that you can be saved by no other than by His great and glorious name. On this account the Lord has sent His angel, who has rule over the beasts, and whose name is Thegri, and has shut up its mouth, so that it cannot tear you. You have escaped from great tribulation on account of your faith, and because you did not doubt in the presence of such a beast. Go, therefore, and tell the elect of the Lord His mighty deeds, and say to them that this beast is a type of the great tribulation that is coming. If then ye prepare yourselves, and repent with all your heart, and turn to the Lord, it will be possible for you to escape it, if your heart be pure and spotless, and ye spend the rest of the days of your life in serving the Lord blamelessly. Cast your cares upon the Lord, and He will direct them. Trust the Lord, ye who doubt, for He is all-powerful, and can turn His anger away from you, and send scourges on the doubters. Woe to those who hear these words, and despise them: better were it for them not to have been born."

CHAP. III

I asked her about the four colours which the beast had on his head. And she answered, and said to me, "Again you are inquisitive in regard to such matters." "Yea, Lady," said I, "make known to me what they are." "Listen," said she: "the black is the world in which we dwell: but the fiery and bloody points out that the world must perish through blood and fire: but the golden part are you who have escaped from this world. For as gold is tested by fire, and thus becomes useful, so are you tested who dwell in it. Those, therefore, who continue stedfast, and are put through the fire, will be purified by means of it. For as gold casts away its dross, so also will ye cast away all sadness and straitness, and will be made pure so as to fit into the building of the tower. But the white part is the age that is to come, in which the elect of God will dwell, since those elected by God to eternal life will be spotless and pure. Wherefore cease not speaking these things into the ears of the saints. This then is the type of the great tribulation that is to come. If ye wish it, it will be nothing. Remember those things which were written down before." And saying this, she departed. But I saw not into what place she retired. There was a noise, however, and I turned round in alarm, thinking that that beast was coming.

Vision Fifth.

Concerning the Commandments.

After I had been praying at home, and had sat down on my couch, there entered a man of glorious aspect, dressed like a shepherd, with a white goat's skin, a wallet on his shoulders, and a rod in his hand, and saluted me. I returned his salutation. And straightway he sat down beside me, and said to me, "I have been sent by a most venerable angel to dwell with you the remaining days of your life." And I thought that he had come to tempt me, and I said to him, "Who are you? For I know him to whom I have been entrusted." He said to me, "Do you not know me?" "No," said I. "I," said he, "am that shepherd to whom you have been entrusted." And while he yet spake, his figure was changed; and then I knew that it was he to whom I had been entrusted. And straightway I became confused, and fear took hold of me, and I was overpowered with deep sorrow that I had answered him so wickedly and foolishly. But he answered, and said to me, "Do not be confounded, but receive strength from the commandments which I am going to give you. For I have been sent," said he, "to show you again all the things which you saw before, especially those of them which are useful to you. First of all, then, write down my commandments and similitudes, and you will write the other things as I shall show you. For this purpose," said he, "I command you to write down the commandments and similitudes first, that you may read them easily, and be able to keep them." Accordingly I wrote down the commandments and similitudes, exactly as he had ordered me. If then, when you have heard these, ye keep them and walk in them, and practice them with pure minds, you will receive from the Lord all that He has promised to you. But if, after you have heard them, ye do not repent, but continue to add to your sins, then shall ye receive from the Lord the opposite things. All these words did the shepherd, even the angel of repentance, command me to write.

Book Second

Commandments

COMMANDMENT FIRST

ON FAITH IN GOD

First of all, believe that there is one God who created and finished all things, and made all things out of nothing. He alone is able to contain the whole, but Himself cannot be contained. Have faith therefore in Him, and fear Him; and fearing Him, exercise self-control. Keep these commands, and you will cast away from you all wickedness, and put on the strength of righteousness, and live to God, if you keep this commandment.

COMMANDMENT SECOND

ON AVOIDING EVIL-SPEAKING, AND ON GIVING ALMS IN SIMPLICITY

He said to me, "Be simple and guileless, and you will be as the children who know not the wickedness that ruins the life of men. First, then, speak evil of no one, nor listen with pleasure to any one who speaks evil of another. But if you listen, you will partake of the sin of him who speaks evil, if you believe the slander which you hear; for believing it, you will also have something to say against your brother. Thus, then, will you be guilty of the sin of him who slanders. For slander is evil and an unsteady demon. It never abides in peace, but always remains in discord. Keep yourself from it, and you will always be at peace with all. Put on a holiness in which there is no wicked cause of offence, but all deeds that are equable and joyful. Practise goodness; and from the rewards of your labours, which God gives you, give to all the needy in simplicity, not hesitating as to whom you are to give or not to give. Give to all, for God wishes His gifts to be shared amongst all. They who receive, will render an account to God why and for what they have received. For the afflicted who receive will not be condemned, but they who receive on false pretences will suffer punishment. He, then, who gives is guiltless. For as he received from the Lord, so has he accomplished his service in simplicity, not hesitating as to whom he should give and to whom he should not give. This service, then, if accomplished in simplicity, is glorious with God. He, therefore, who thus ministers in simplicity, will live to God. Keep therefore these commandments, as I have given them to you, that your repentance and the repentance of your house may be found in simplicity, and your heart may be pure and stainless."

COMMANDMENT THIRD

ON AVOIDING FALSEHOOD, AND ON THE REPENTANCE OF HERMAS FOR HIS DISSIMULATION

Again he said to me, "Love the truth, and let nothing but truth proceed from your mouth, that the spirit which God has placed in your flesh may be found truthful before all men; and the Lord, who dwelleth in you, will be glorified, because the Lord is truthful in every word, and in Him is no falsehood. They therefore who lie deny the Lord, and rob Him, not giving back to Him the deposit which they have received. For they received from Him a spirit free from falsehood. If they give him back this spirit untruthful, they pollute the commandment of the Lord, and become robbers." On hearing these words, I wept most violently. When he saw me weeping, he said to me, "Why do you weep?" And I said, "Because, sir, I know not if I can be saved." "Why?" said he. And I said, "Because, sir, I never spake a true word in my life, but have ever spoken cunningly to all, and have affirmed a lie for the truth to all; and no one ever contradicted me, but credit was given to my word. How then can I live, since I have acted thus?" And he said to me, "Your feelings are indeed right and sound, for you ought as a servant of God to have walked in truth, and not to have joined an evil conscience with the spirit of truth, nor to have caused sadness to the holy and true Spirit." And I said to him, "Never, sir, did I listen to these words with so much attention." And he said to me, "Now you hear them, and keep them, that even the falsehoods which you formerly told in your transactions may come to be believed through the truthfulness of your present statements. For even they can become worthy of credit. If you keep these precepts, and from this time forward you speak nothing but the truth, it will be possible for you to obtain life. And whosoever shall hear this commandment, and depart from that great wickedness falsehood, shall live to God."

COMMANDMENT FOURTH

ON PUTTING ONE'S WIFE AWAY FOR ADULTERY

CHAP. I

"I charge you," said he, "to guard your chastity, and let no thought enter your heart of another man's wife, or of fornication, or of similar iniquities; for by doing this you commit a great sin. But if you always remember your own wife, you will never sin. For if this thought enter your heart, then you will sin; and if, in like manner, you think other wicked thoughts, you commit sin. For this thought is great sin in a servant of God. But if any one commit this wicked deed, he works death for himself. Attend, therefore, and refrain from this thought; for where purity dwells, there iniquity ought not to enter the heart of a righteous man." I said to him, "Sir, permit me to ask you a few questions." "Say on," said he. And I said to him, "Sir, if any one has a wife who trusts in the Lord, and if he detect her in adultery, does the man sin if he continue to live with her?" And he said to me, "As long as he remains ignorant of her sin, the husband commits no transgression in living with her. But if the husband know that his wife has gone astray, and if the woman does not repent, but persists in her fornication, and yet the husband continues to live with her, he also is guilty of her crime, and a sharer in her adultery." And I said to him, "What then, sir, is the husband to do, if his wife continue in her vicious practices?" And he said, "The husband should put her away, and remain by himself. But if he put his wife away and marry another, he also commits adultery." And I said to him, "What if the woman put away should repent, and wish to return to her husband: shall she not be taken back by her husband?" And he said to me, "Assuredly. If the husband do not take her back, he sins, and brings a great sin upon himself; for he ought to take back the sinner who has repented. But not frequently. For there is but one repentance to the servants of God.

In case, therefore, that the divorced wife may repent, the husband ought not to marry another, when his wife has been put away. In this matter man and woman are to be treated exactly in the same way. Moreover, adultery is committed not only by those who pollute their flesh, but by those who imitate the heathen in their actions. Wherefore if any one persists in such deeds, and repents not, withdraw from him, and cease to live with him, otherwise you are a sharer in his sin. Therefore has the injunction been laid on you, that you should remain by yourselves, both man and woman, for in such persons repentance can take place. But I do not," said he, "give opportunity for the doing of these deeds, but that he who has sinned may sin no more. But with regard to his previous transgressions, there is One who is able to provide a cure; for it is He, indeed, who has power over all."

CHAP. II

I asked him again, and said, "Since the Lord has vouchsafed to dwell always with me, bear with me while I utter a few words; for I understand nothing, and my heart has been hardened by my previous mode of life. Give me understanding, for I am exceedingly dull, and I understand absolutely nothing." And he answered and said unto me, "I am set over repentance, and I give understanding to all who repent. Do you not think," he said, "that it is great wisdom to repent? for repentance is great wisdom. For he who has sinned understands that he acted wickedly in the sight of the Lord, and remembers the actions he has done, and he repents, and no longer acts wickedly, but does good munificently, and humbles and torments his soul because he has sinned. You see, therefore, that repentance is great wisdom." And I said to him, "It is for this reason, sir, that I inquire carefully into all things, especially because I am a sinner; that I may know what works I should do, that I may live: for my sins are many and various." And he said to me, "You shall live if you keep my commandments, and walk in them; and whosoever shall hear and keep these commandments, shall live to God."

CHAP. III

And I said to him, "I should like to continue my questions." "Speak on," said he. And I said, "I heard, sir, some teachers maintain that there is no other repentance than that which takes place, when we descended into the water and received remission of our former sins." He said to me, "That was sound doctrine which you heard; for that is really the case. For he who has received remission of his sins ought not to sin any more, but to live in purity. Since, however, you inquire diligently into all things, I will point this also out to you, not as giving occasion for error to those who are to believe, or have lately believed, in the Lord. For those who have now believed, and those who are to believe, have not repentance for their sins; but they have remission of their previous sins. For to those who have been called before these days, the Lord has set repentance. For the Lord, knowing the heart, and foreknowing all things, knew the weakness of men and the manifold wiles of the devil, that he would inflict some evil on the servants of God, and would act wickedly towards them. The Lord, therefore, being merciful, has had mercy on the work of His hand, and has set repentance for them; and He has entrusted to me power over this repentance. And therefore I say to you, that if any one is tempted by the devil, and sins after that great and holy calling in which the Lord has called His people to everlasting life, he has opportunity to repent but once. But if he should sin frequently after this, and then repent, to such a man his repentance will be of no avail; for with difficulty will he live." And I said, "Sir, I feel that life has come back to me in listening attentively to these commandments; for I know that I shall be saved, if in future I sin no more." And he said, "You will be saved, you and all who keep these commandments."

CHAP. IV

And again I asked him, saying, "Sir, since you have been so patient in listening to me, will you show me this also?" "Speak," said he. And I said, "If a wife or husband die, and the widower or widow marry, does he or she commit sin?" "There is no sin in marrying again," said he; "but if they remain unmarried, they gain greater honour and glory with the Lord; but if they marry, they do not sin. Guard, therefore, your chastity and purity, and you will live to God. What commandments I now give you, and what I am to give, keep from henceforth, yea, from the very day when you were entrusted to me, and I will dwell in your house. And your former sins will be forgiven, if you keep my commandments. And all shall be forgiven who keep these my commandments, and walk in this chastity."

COMMANDMENT FIFTH

OF SADNESS OF HEART, AND OF PATIENCE

CHAP. I

"Be patient," said he, "and of good understanding, and you will rule over every wicked work, and you will work all righteousness. For if you be patient, the Holy Spirit that dwells in you will be pure. He will not be darkened by any evil spirit, but, dwelling in a broad region, he will rejoice and be glad; and with the vessel in which he dwells he will serve God in gladness, having great peace within himself. But if any outburst of anger take place, forthwith the Holy Spirit, who is tender, is straitened, not having a pure place, and He seeks to depart. For he is choked by the vile spirit, and cannot attend on the Lord as he wishes, for anger pollutes him. For the Lord dwells in long-suffering, but the devil in anger. The two spirits, then, when dwelling in the same habitation, are at discord with each other, and are troublesome to that man in whom they dwell. For if an exceedingly small piece of wormwood be taken and put into a jar of honey, is not the honey entirely destroyed, and does not the exceedingly small piece of wormwood entirely take away the sweetness of the honey, so that it no longer affords any gratification to its owner, but has become bitter, and lost its use? But if the wormwood be not put into the honey, then the honey remains sweet, and is of use to its owner. You see, then, that patience is sweeter than honey, and useful to God, and the Lord dwells in it. But anger is bitter and useless. Now, if anger be mingled with patience, the patience is polluted, and its prayer is not then useful to God." "I should like, sir," said I, "to know the power of anger, that I may guard myself against it." And he said, "If you do not guard yourself against it, you and your house lose all hope of salvation. Guard yourself, therefore, against it. For I am with you, and all will depart from it who repent with their whole heart. For I will be with them, and I will save them all. For all are justified by the most holy angel."

CHAP. II

"Hear now," said he, "how wicked is the action of anger, and in what way it overthrows the servants of God by its action, and turns them from righteousness. But it does not turn away those who are full of faith, nor does it act on them, for the power of the Lord is with them. It is the thoughtless and doubting that it turns away. For as soon as it sees such men standing stedfast, it throws itself into their hearts, and for nothing at all the man or woman becomes embittered on account of occurrences in their daily life, as for instance on account of their food, or some superfluous word that has been uttered, or on account of some friend, or some gift or debt, or some such senseless affair. For all these things are foolish and empty and unprofitable to the servants of God. But patience is great, and mighty, and strong, and calm in the midst of great enlargement, joyful, rejoicing, free from care, glorifying God at all times, having no bitterness in her, and abiding continually meek and quiet. Now this patience dwells with those who have complete faith. But anger is foolish, and fickle, and senseless. Now, of folly is begotten bitterness, and of bitterness anger, and of anger frenzy. This frenzy, the product of so many evils, ends in great and incurable sin. For when all these spirits dwell in one vessel in which the Holy Spirit also dwells, the vessel cannot contain them, but overflows. The tender Spirit, then, not being accustomed to dwell with the wicked spirit, nor with hardness, withdraws from such a man, and seeks to dwell with meekness and peacefulness. Then, when he withdraws from the man in whom he dwelt, the man is emptied of the righteous Spirit; and being henceforward filled with evil spirits, he is in a state of anarchy in every action, being dragged hither and thither by the evil spirits, and there is a complete darkness in his mind as to everything good. This, then, is what happens to all the angry. Wherefore do you depart from that most wicked spirit anger, and put on patience, and resist anger and bitterness, and you will be found in company with the purity which is loved by the Lord. Take care, then, that you neglect not by any chance this commandment: for if you obey this commandment, you will be able to keep all the other commandments which I am to give you. Be strong, then, in these commandments, and put on power, and let all put on power, as many as wish to walk in them."

COMMANDMENT SIXTH

HOW TO RECOGNISE THE TWO SPIRITS ATTENDANT ON EACH MAN, AND HOW TO DISTINGUISH THE SUGGESTIONS OF THE ONE FROM THOSE OF THE OTHER

CHAP. I

"I gave you," he said, "directions in the first commandment to attend to faith, and fear, and self-restraint." "Even so, sir," said I. And he said, "Now I wish to show you the powers of these, that you may know what power each possesses. For their powers are double, and have relation alike to the righteous and the unrighteous. Trust you, therefore, the righteous, but put no trust in the unrighteous. For the path of righteousness is straight, but that of unrighteousness is crooked. But walk in the straight and even way, and mind not the crooked. For the crooked path has no roads, but has many pathless places and stumbling-blocks in it, and it is rough and thorny. It is injurious to those who walk therein. But they who walk in the straight road walk evenly without stumbling, because it is neither rough nor thorny. You see, then, that it is better to walk in this road." "I wish to go by this road," said I. "You will go by it," said he; "and whoever turns to the Lord with all his heart will walk in it."

CHAP. II

"Hear now," said he, "in regard to faith. There are two angels with a man—one of righteousness, and the other of iniquity." And I said to him, "How, sir, am I to know the powers of these, for both angels dwell with me?" "Hear," said he, and "understand them. The angel of righteousness is gentle and modest, meek and peaceful. When, therefore, he ascends into your heart, forthwith he talks to you of righteousness, purity, chastity, contentment, and of every righteous deed and glorious virtue. When all these ascend into your heart, know that the angel of righteousness is with you. These are the deeds of the angel of righteousness. Trust him, then, and his works. Look now at the works of the angel of iniquity. First, he is wrathful, and bitter, and foolish, and his works are evil, and ruin the servants of God. When, then, he ascends into your heart, know him by his works." And I said to him, "How, sir, I shall perceive him, I do not know." "Hear and understand" said he. "When anger comes upon you, or harshness, know that he is in you; and you will know this to be the case also, when you are attacked by a longing after many transactions, and the richest delicacies, and drunken revels, and divers luxuries, and things improper, and by a hankering after women, and by overreaching, and pride, and blustering, and by whatever is like to these. When these ascend into your heart, know that the angel of iniquity is in you. Now that you know his works, depart from him, and in no respect trust him, because his deeds are evil, and unprofitable to the servants of God. These, then, are the actions of both angels. Understand them, and trust the angel of righteousness; but depart from the angel of iniquity, because his instruction is bad in every deed. For though a man be most faithful, and the thought of this angel ascend into his heart, that man or woman must sin. On the other hand, be a man or woman ever so bad, yet, if the works of the angel of righteousness ascend into his or her heart, he or she must do something good. You see, therefore, that it is good to follow the angel of righteousness, but to bid farewell to the angel of iniquity."

"This commandment exhibits the deeds of faith, that you may trust the works of the angel of righteousness, and doing them you may live to God. But believe the works of the angel of iniquity are hard. If you refuse to do them, you will live to God."

COMMANDMENT SEVENTH

ON FEARING GOD, AND NOT FEARING THE DEVIL

"Fear," said he, "the Lord, and keep His commandments. For if you keep the commandments of God, you will be powerful in every action, and every one of your actions will be incomparable. For, fearing the Lord, you will do all things well. This is the fear which you ought to have, that you may be saved. But fear not the devil; for, fearing the Lord, you will have dominion over the devil, for there is no power in him. But he in whom there is no power ought on no account to be an object of fear; but He in whom there is glorious power is truly to be feared. For every one that has power ought to be feared; but he who has not power is despised by all. Fear, therefore, the deeds of the devil, since they are wicked. For, fearing the Lord, you will not do these deeds, but will refrain from them. For fears are of two kinds: for if you do not wish to do that which is evil, fear the Lord, and you will not do it; but, again, if you wish to do that which is good, fear the Lord, and you will do it. Wherefore the fear of the Lord is strong, and great, and glorious. Fear, then, the Lord, and you will live to Him, and as many as fear Him and keep His commandments will live to God." "Why," said I, "sir, did you say in regard to those that keep His commandments, that they will live to God?" "Because," says he, "all creation fears the Lord, but all creation does not keep His commandments. They only who fear the Lord and keep His commandments have life with God; but as to those who keep not His commandments, there is no life in them."

COMMANDMENT EIGHTH

WE OUGHT TO SHUN THAT WHICH IS EVIL, AND DO THAT WHICH IS GOOD

"I told you," said he, "that the creatures of God are double, for restraint also is double; for in some cases restraint has to be exercised, in others there is no need of restraint." "Make known to me, sir," say I, "in what cases restraint has to be exercised, and in what cases it has not." "Restrain yourself in regard to evil, and do it not; but exercise no restraint in regard to good, but do it. For if you exercise restraint in the doing of good, you will commit a great sin; but if you exercise restraint, so as not to do that which is evil, you are practising great righteousness. Restrain yourself, therefore, from all iniquity, and do that which is good." "What, sir," say I, "are the evil deeds from which we must restrain ourselves?" "Hear," says he: "from adultery and fornication, from unlawful revelling, from wicked luxury, from indulgence in many kinds of food and the extravagance of riches, and from boastfulness, and haughtiness, and insolence, and lies, and backbiting, and hypocrisy, from the remembrance of wrong, and from all slander. These are the deeds that are most wicked in the life of men. From all these deeds, therefore, the servant of God must restrain himself. For he who does not restrain himself from these, cannot live to God. Listen, then, to the deeds that accompany these." "Are there, sir," said I, "any other evil deeds?" "There are," says he; "and many of them, too, from which the servant of God must restrain himself—theft, lying, robbery, false witness, overreaching, wicked lust, deceit, vainglory, boastfulness, and all other vices like to these." "Do you not think that these are really wicked?" "Exceedingly wicked in the servants of God. From all of these the servant of God must restrain himself. Restrain yourself, then, from all these, that you may live to God, and you will be enrolled amongst those who restrain themselves in regard to these matters. These, then, are the things from which you must restrain yourself."

"But listen," says he, "to the things in regard to which you have not to exercise self-restraint, but which you ought to do. Restrain not yourself in regard to that which is good, but do it." "And tell me, sir," say I, "the nature of the good deeds, that I may walk in them and wait on them, so that doing them I can be saved." "Listen," says he, "to the good deeds which you ought to do, and in regard to which there is no self-restraint requisite. First of all there is faith, then fear of the Lord, love, concord, words of righteousness, truth, patience. Than these, nothing is better in the life of men. If any one attend to these, and restrain himself not from them, blessed is he in his life. Then there are the following attendant on these: helping widows, looking after orphans and the needy, rescuing the servants of God from necessities, the being hospitable—for in hospitality good-doing finds a field—never opposing any one, the being quiet, having fewer needs than all men, reverencing the aged, practising righteousness, watching the brotherhood, bearing insolence, being long-suffering, encouraging those who are sick in soul, not casting those who have fallen into sin from the faith, but turning them back and restoring them to peace of mind, admonishing sinners, not oppressing debtors and the needy, and if there are any other actions like these. Do these seem to you good?" says he. "For what, sir," say I, "is better than these?" "Walk then in them," says he, "and restrain not yourself from them, and you will live to God. Keep, therefore, this commandment. If you do good, and restrain not yourself from it, you will live to God. All who act thus will live to God. And, again, if you refuse to do evil, and restrain yourself from it, you will live to God. And all will live to God who keep these commandments, and walk in them."

COMMANDMENT NINTH

PRAYER MUST BE MADE TO GOD WITHOUT CEASING, AND WITH UNWAVERING CONFIDENCE

He says to me, "Put away doubting from you and do not hesitate to ask of the Lord, saying to yourself, How can I ask of the Lord and receive from Him, seeing I have sinned so much against Him? Do not thus reason with yourself, but with all your heart turn to the Lord and ask of Him without doubting, and you will know the multitude of His tender mercies; that He will never leave you, but fulfil the request of your soul. For He is not like men, who remember evils done against them; but He Himself remembers not evils, and has compassion on His own creature. Cleanse, therefore, your heart from all the vanities of this world, and from the words already mentioned, and ask of the Lord and you will receive all, and in none of your requests will you be denied which you make to the Lord without doubting. But if you doubt in your heart, you will receive none of your requests. For those who doubt regarding God are double-souled, and obtain not one of their requests. But those who are perfect in faith ask everything, trusting in the Lord; and they obtain, because they ask nothing doubting, and not being double-souled. For every double-souled man, even if he repent, will with difficulty be saved. Cleanse your heart, therefore, from all doubt, and put on faith, because it is strong, and trust God that you will obtain from Him all that you ask. And if at any time, after you have asked of the Lord, you are slower in obtaining your request [than you expected], do not doubt because you have not soon obtained the request of your soul; for invariably it is on account of some temptation or some sin of which you are ignorant that you are slower in obtaining your request. Wherefore do not cease to make the request of your soul, and you will obtain it. But if you grow weary and waver in your request, blame yourself, and not Him who does not give to you. Consider this doubting state of mind, for it is wicked and senseless, and turns many away entirely from the faith, even though they be very strong. For this doubting is the daughter of the devil, and acts exceedingly wickedly to the servants of God. Despise, then, doubting, and gain the mastery over it in everything; clothing yourself with faith, which is strong and powerful. For faith promises all things, perfects all things; but doubt having no thorough faith in itself, fails in every work which it undertakes. You see, then," says he, "that, faith is from above—from the Lord—and has great power; but doubt is an earthly spirit, coming from the devil, and has no power. Serve, then, that which has power, namely faith, and keep away from doubt, which has no power, and you will live to God. And all will live to God whose minds have been set on these things."

COMMANDMENT TENTH

OF GRIEF, AND NOT GRIEVING THE SPIRIT OF GOD WHICH IS IN US

CHAP. I

"Remove from you," says he, "grief; for she is the sister of doubt and anger." "How, sir," say I, "is she the sister of these? for anger, doubt, and grief seem to be quite different from each other." "You are senseless, O man. Do you not perceive that grief is more wicked than all the spirits, and most terrible to the servants of God, and more than all other spirits destroys man and crushes out the Holy Spirit, and yet, on the other hand, she saves him?" "I am senseless, sir," say I, "and do not understand these parables. For how she can crush out, and on the other hand save, I do not perceive." "Listen," says he. "Those who have never searched for the truth, nor investigated the nature of the Divinity, but have simply believed, when they devote themselves to and become mixed up with business, and wealth, and heathen friendships, and many other actions of this world, do not perceive the parables of Divinity; for their minds are darkened by these actions, and they are corrupted and become dried up. Even as beautiful vines, when they are neglected, are withered up by thorns and divers plants, so men who have believed, and have afterwards fallen away into many of those actions above mentioned, go astray in their minds, and lose all understanding in regard to righteousness; for if they hear of righteousness, their minds are occupied with their business, and they give no heed at all. Those, on the other hand, who have the fear of God, and search after Godhead and truth, and have their hearts turned to the Lord, quickly perceive and understand what is said to them, because they have the fear of the Lord in them. For where the Lord dwells, there is much understanding. Cleave, then, to the Lord, and you will understand and perceive all things."

CHAP. II

"Hear, then," says he, "foolish man, how grief crushes out the Holy Spirit, and on the other hand saves. When the doubting man attempts any deed, and fails in it on account of his doubt, this grief enters into the man, and grieves the Holy Spirit, and crushes him out. Then, on the other hand, when anger attaches itself to a man in regard to any matter, and he is embittered, then grief enters into the heart of the man who was irritated, and he is grieved at the deed which he did, and repents that he has wrought a wicked deed. This grief, then, appears to be accompanied by salvation, because the man, after having done a wicked deed, repented. Both actions grieve the Spirit: doubt, because it did not accomplish its object; and anger grieves the Spirit, because it did what was wicked. Both these are grievous to the Holy Spirit—doubt and anger. Wherefore remove grief from you, and crush not the Holy Spirit which dwells in you, lest he entreat God against you, and he withdraw from you. For the Spirit of God which has been granted to us to dwell in this body does not endure grief nor straitness. Wherefore put on cheerfulness, which always is agreeable and acceptable to God, and rejoice in it. For every cheerful man does what is good, and minds what is good, and despises grief; but the sorrowful man always acts wickedly. First, he acts wickedly because he grieves the Holy Spirit, which was given to man a cheerful Spirit. Secondly, Grieving the Holy Spirit, he works iniquity, neither entreating the Lord nor confessing to Him. For the entreaty of the sorrowful man has no power to ascend to the altar of God." "Why," say I, "does not the entreaty of the grieved man ascend to the altar?" "Because," says he, "grief sits in his heart. Grief, then, mingled with his entreaty, does not permit the entreaty to ascend pure to the altar of God. For as vinegar and wine, when mixed in the same vessel, do not give the same pleasure [as wine alone gives], so grief mixed with the Holy Spirit does not produce the same entreaty [as would be produced by the Holy Spirit alone]. Cleanse yourself from this wicked grief, and you will live to God; and all will live to God who drive away grief from them, and put on all cheerfulness."

COMMANDMENT ELEVENTH

THE SPIRIT AND PROPHETS TO BE TRIED BY THEIR WORKS; ALSO OF THE TWO KINDS OF SPIRIT

He pointed out to me some men sitting on a seat, and one man sitting on a chair. And he says to me, "Do you see the persons sitting on the seat?" "I do, sir," said I. "These," says he, "are the faithful, and he who sits on the chair is a false prophet, ruining the minds of the servants of God. It is the doubters, not the faithful, that he ruins. These doubters then go to him as to a soothsayer, and inquire of him what will happen to them; and he, the false prophet, not having the power of a Divine Spirit in him, answers them according to their inquiries, and according to their wicked desires, and fills their souls with expectations, according to their own wishes. For being himself empty, he gives empty answers to empty inquirers; for every answer is made to the emptiness of man. Some true words he does occasionally utter; for the devil fills him with his own spirit, in the hope that he may be able to overcome some of the righteous. As many, then, as are strong in the faith of the Lord, and are clothed with truth, have no connection with such spirits, but keep away from them; but as many as are of doubtful minds and frequently repent, betake themselves to soothsaying, even as the heathen, and bring greater sin upon themselves by their idolatry. For he who inquires of a false prophet in regard to any action is an idolater, and devoid of the truth, and foolish. For no spirit given by God requires to be asked; but such a spirit having the power of Divinity speaks all things of itself, for it proceeds from above from the power of the Divine Spirit. But the spirit which is asked and speaks according to the desires of men is earthly, light, and powerless, and it is altogether silent if it is not questioned." "How then, sir," say I, "will a man know which of them is the prophet, and which the false prophet?" "I will tell you," says he, "about both the prophets, and then you can try the true and the false prophet according to my directions. Try the man who has the Divine Spirit by his life. First, he who has the Divine Spirit proceeding from above is meek, and peaceable, and humble, and refrains from all iniquity and the vain desire of this world, and contents himself with fewer wants than those of other men, and when asked he makes no reply; nor does he speak privately, nor when man wishes the spirit to speak does the Holy Spirit speak, but it speaks only when God wishes it to speak. When, then, a man having the Divine Spirit comes into an assembly of righteous men who have faith in the Divine Spirit, and this assembly of men offers up prayer to God, then the angel of the prophetic Spirit, who is destined for him, fills the man; and the man being filled with the Holy Spirit, speaks to the multitude as the Lord wishes. Thus, then, will the Spirit of Divinity become manifest. Whatever power therefore comes from the Spirit of Divinity belongs to the Lord. Hear, then," says he, "in regard to the spirit which is earthly, and empty, and powerless, and foolish. First, the man who seems to have the Spirit exalts himself, and wishes to have the first seat, and is bold, and impudent, and talkative, and lives in the midst of many luxuries and many other delusions, and takes rewards for his prophecy; and if he does not receive rewards, he does not prophesy. Can, then, the Divine Spirit take rewards and prophesy? It is not possible that the prophet of God should do this, but prophets of this character are possessed by an earthly spirit. Then it never approaches an assembly of righteous men, but shuns them. And it associates with doubters and the vain, and prophesies to them in a corner, and deceives them, speaking to them, according to their desires, mere empty words: for they are empty to whom it gives its answers. For the empty vessel, when placed along with the empty, is not crushed, but they correspond to each other. When, therefore, it comes into an assembly of righteous men who have a Spirit of Divinity, and they offer up prayer, that man is made empty, and the earthly spirit tees from him through fear, and that man is made dumb, and is entirely crushed, being unable to speak. For if you pack closely a storehouse with wine or oil, and put an empty jar in the midst of the vessels of wine or oil, you will find that jar empty as when you placed it, if you should wish to clear the storehouse. So also the empty prophets, when they come to the spirits of the righteous, are found [on leaving] to be such as they were when they came. This, then, is the mode of life of both prophets. Try by his deeds and his life the man who says that he is inspired. But as for you, trust the Spirit which comes from God, and has power; but the spirit which is earthly and empty trust not at all, for there is no power in it: it comes from the devil. Hear, then, the parable which I am to tell you. Take a stone, and throw it to the sky, and see if you can touch it. Or again, take a squirt of water and squirt into the sky, and see if you can penetrate the sky." "How, sir," say I, "can these things take place? for both of them are impossible." "As these things," says he, "are impossible, so also are the earthly spirits powerless and pithless. But look, on the other hand, at the power which comes from above. Hail is of the size of a very small grain, yet when it falls on a man's head how much annoyance it gives him! Or, again, take the drop which falls from a pitcher to the ground, and yet it hollows a stone. You see, then, that the smallest things coming from above have great power when they fall upon the earth. Thus also is the Divine Spirit, which comes from above, powerful. Trust, then, that Spirit, but have nothing to do with the other."

COMMANDMENT TWELFTH

ON THE TWOFOLD DESIRE. THE COMMANDMENTS OF GOD CAN BE KEPT, AND BELIEVERS OUGHT NOT TO FEAR THE DEVIL

CHAP. I

He says to me, "Put away from you all wicked desire, and clothe yourself with good and chaste desire; for clothed with this desire you will hate wicked desire, and will rein yourself in even as you wish. For wicked desire is wild, and is with difficulty tamed. For it is terrible, and consumes men exceedingly by its wildness. Especially is the servant of God terribly consumed by it, if he falls into it and is devoid of understanding. Moreover, it consumes all such as have not on them the garment of good desire, but are entangled and mixed up with this world. These it delivers up to death." "What then, sir," say I, "are the deeds of wicked desire which deliver men over to death? Make them known to me, and I will refrain from them." "Listen, then, to the works in which evil desire slays the servants of God."

CHAP. II

"Foremost of all is the desire after another's wife or husband, and after extravagance, and many useless dainties and drinks, and many other foolish luxuries; for all luxury is foolish and empty in the servants of God. These, then, are the evil desires which slay the servants of God. For this evil desire is the daughter of the devil. You must refrain from evil desires, that by refraining ye may live to God. But as many as are mastered by them, and do not resist them, will perish at last, for these desires are fatal. Put you on, then, the desire of righteousness; and arming yourself with the fear of the Lord, resist them. For the fear of the Lord dwells in good desire. But if evil desire see you armed with the fear of God, and resisting it, it will flee far from you, and it will no longer appear to you, for it fears your armour. Go, then, garlanded with the crown which you have gained for victory over it, to the desire of righteousness, and, delivering up to it the prize which you have received, serve it even as it wishes. If you serve good desire, and be subject to it, you will gain the mastery over evil desire, and make it subject to you even as you wish."

CHAP. III

"I should like to know," say I, "in what way I ought to serve good desire." "Hear," says he: "You will practice righteousness and virtue, truth and the fear of the Lord, faith and meekness, and whatsoever excellences are like to these. Practising these, you will be a well-pleasing servant of God, and you will live to Him; and every one who shall serve good desire, shall live to God."

He concluded the twelve commandments, and said to me, "You have now these commandments. Walk in them, and exhort your hearers that their repentance may be pure during the remainder of their life. Fulfil carefully this ministry which I now entrust to you, and you will accomplish much. For you will find favour among those who are to repent, and they will give heed to your words; for I will be with you, and will compel them to obey you." I say to him, "Sir, these commandments are great, and good, and glorious, and fitted to gladden the heart of the man who can perform them. But I do not know if these commandments can be kept by man, because they are exceeding hard." He answered and said to me, "If you lay it down as certain that they can be kept, then you will easily keep them, and they will not be hard. But if you come to imagine that they cannot be kept by man, then you will not keep them. Now I say to you, If you do not keep them, but neglect them, you will not be saved, nor your children, nor your house, since you have already determined for yourself that these commandments cannot be kept by man."

CHAP. IV

These things he said to me in tones of the deepest anger, so that I was confounded and exceedingly afraid of him, for his figure was altered so that a man could not endure his anger. But seeing me altogether agitated and confused, he began to speak to me in more gentle tones; and he said: "O fool, senseless and doubting, do you not perceive how great is the glory of God, and how strong and marvellous, in that He created the world for the sake of man, and subjected all creation to him, and gave him power to rule over everything under heaven? If, then, man is lord of the creatures of God, and rules over all, is he not able to be lord also of these commandments? For," says he, "the man who has the Lord in his heart can also be lord of all, and of every one of these commandments. But to those who have the Lord only on their lips, but their hearts hardened, and who are far from the Lord, the commandments are hard and difficult. Put, therefore, ye who are empty and fickle in your faith, the Lord in your heart, and ye will know that there is nothing easier or sweeter, or more manageable, than these commandments. Return, ye who walk in the commandments of the devil, in hard, and bitter, and wild licentiousness, and fear not the devil; for there is no power in him against you, for I will be with you, the angel of repentance, who am lord over him. The devil has fear only, but his fear has no strength. Fear him not, then, and he will flee from you."

CHAP. V

I say to him, "Sir, listen to me for a moment." "Say what you wish," says he. "Man, sir," say I, "is eager to keep the commandments of God, and there is no one who does not ask of the Lord that strength may be given him for these commandments, and that he may be subject to them; but the devil is hard, and holds sway over them." "He cannot," says he, "hold sway over the servants of God, who with all their heart place their hopes in Him. The devil can wrestle against these, overthrow them he cannot. If, then, ye resist him, he will be conquered, and flee in disgrace from you. As many, therefore," says he, "as are empty, fear the devil, as possessing power. When a man has filled very suitable jars with good wine, and a few among those jars are left empty, then he comes to the jars, and does not look at the full jars, for he knows that they are full; but he looks at the empty, being afraid lest they have become sour. For empty jars quickly become sour, and the goodness of the wine is gone. So also the devil goes to all the servants of God to try them. As many, then, as are full in the faith, resist him strongly, and he withdraws from them, having no way by which he might enter them. He goes, then, to the empty, and finding a way of entrance, into them, he produces in them whatever he wishes, and they become his servants."

CHAP. VI

"But I, the angel of repentance, say to you Fear not the devil; for I was sent," says he, "to be with you who repent with all your heart, and to make you strong in faith. Trust God, then, ye who on account of your sins have despaired of life, and who add to your sins and weigh down your life; for if ye return to the Lord with all your heart, and practice righteousness the rest of your days, and serve Him according to His will, He will heal your former sins, and you will have power to hold sway over the works of the devil. But as to the threats of the devil, fear them not at all, for he is powerless as the sinews of a dead man. Give ear to me, then, and fear Him who has all power, both to save and destroy, and keep His commandments, and ye will live to God." I say to him, "Sir, I am now made strong in all the ordinances of the Lord, because you are with me; and I know that you will crush all the power of the devil, and we shall have rule over him, and shall prevail against all his works. And I hope, sir, to be able to keep all these commandments which you have enjoined upon me, the Lord strengthening me." "You will keep them," says he, "if your heart be pure towards the Lord; and all will keep them who cleanse their hearts from the vain desires of this world, and they will live to God."

Book Third

Similitudes

SIMILITUDE FIRST

AS IN THIS WORLD WE HAVE NO ABIDING CITY, WE OUGHT TO SEEK ONE TO COME

He says to me, "You know that you who are the servants of God dwell in a strange land; for your city is far away from this one. If, then," he continues, "you know your city in which you are to dwell, why do ye here provide lands, and make expensive preparations, and accumulate dwellings and useless buildings? He who makes such preparations for this city cannot return again to his own. Oh foolish, and unstable, and miserable man! Dost thou not understand that all these things belong to another, and are under the power of another? for the lord of this city will say, I do not wish thee to dwell in my city; but depart from this city, because thou obeyest not my laws.' Thou, therefore, although having fields and houses, and many other things, when cast out by him, what wilt thou do with thy land, and house, and other possessions which thou hast gathered to thyself? For the lord of this country justly says to thee, Either obey my laws or depart from my dominion.' What, then, dost thou intend to do, having a law in thine own city, on account of thy lands, and the rest of thy possessions? Thou shalt altogether deny thy law, and walk according to the law of this city. See lest it be to thy hurt to deny thy law; for if thou shalt desire to return to thy city, thou wilt not be received, because thou hast denied the law of thy city, but wilt be excluded from it. Have a care, therefore: as one living in a foreign land, make no further preparations for thyself than such merely as may be sufficient; and be ready, when the master of this city shall come to cast thee out for disobeying his law, to leave his city, and to depart to thine own, and to obey thine own law without being exposed to annoyance, but in great joy. Have a care, then, ye who serve the Lord, and have Him in your heart, that ye work the works of God, remembering His commandments and promises which He promised, and believe that He will bring them to pass if His commandments be observed. Instead of lands, therefore, buy afflicted souls, according as each one is able, and visit widows and orphans, and do not overlook them; and spend your wealth and all your preparations, which ye received from the Lord, upon such lands and houses. For to this end did the Master make you rich, that you might perform these services unto Him; and it is much better to purchase such lands, and possessions, and houses, as you will find in your own city, when you come to reside in it. This is a noble and sacred expenditure, attended neither with sorrow nor fear, but with joy. Do not practice the expenditure of the heathen, for it is injurious to you who are the servants of God; but practice an expenditure of your own, in which ye can rejoice; and do not corrupt nor touch what is another's nor covet it, for it is an evil thing to covet the goods of other men; but work thine own work, and thou wilt be saved."

SIMILITUDE SECOND

AS THE VINE IS SUPPORTED BY THE ELM, SO IS THE RICH MAN HELPED BY THE PRAYER OF THE POOR

As I was walking in the field, and observing an elm and vine, and determining in my own mind respecting them and their fruits, the Shepherd appears to me, and says, "What is it that you are thinking about the elm and vine?" "I am considering," I reply, "that they become each other exceedingly well." "These two trees," he continues, "are intended as an example for the servants of God." "I would like to know," said I, "the example which these trees you say, are intended to teach." "Do you see," he says, "the elm and the vine?" "I see them sir," I replied. "This vine," he continued, "produces fruit, and the elm is an unfruitful tree; but unless the vine be trained upon the elm, it cannot bear much fruit when extended at length upon the ground; and the fruit which it does bear is rotten, because the plant is not suspended upon the elm. When, therefore, the vine is cast upon the elm, it yields fruit both from itself and from the elm. You see, moreover, that the elm also produces much fruit, not less than the vine, but even more; because," he continued, "the vine, when suspended upon the elm, yields much fruit, and good; but when thrown upon the ground, what it produces is small and rotten. This similitude, therefore, is for the servants of God—for the poor man and for the rich." "How so, sir?" said I; "explain the matter to me." "Listen," he said: "The rich man has much wealth, but is poor in matters relating to the Lord, because he is distracted about his riches; and he offers very few confessions and intercessions to the Lord, and those which he does offer are small and weak, and have no power above. But when the rich man refreshes the poor, and assists him in his necessities, believing that what he does to the poor man will be able to find its reward with God—because the poor man is rich in intercession and confession, and his intercession has great power with God—then the rich man helps the poor in all things without hesitation; and the poor man, being helped by the rich, intercedes for him, giving thanks to God for him who bestows gifts upon him. And he still continues to interest himself zealously for the poor man, that his wants may be constantly supplied. For he knows that the intercession of the poor man is acceptable and influential with God. Both, accordingly, accomplish their work. The poor man makes intercession; a work in which he is rich, which he received from the Lord, and with which he recompenses the master who helps him. And the rich man, in like manner, unhesitatingly bestows upon the poor man the riches which he received from the Lord. And this is a great work, and acceptable before God, because he understands the object of his wealth, and has given to the poor of the gifts of the Lord, and rightly discharged his service to Him. Among men, however, the elm appears not to produce fruit, and they do not know nor understand that if a drought come, the elm, which contains water, nourishes the vine; and the vine, having an unfailing supply of water, yields double fruit both for itself and for the elm. So also poor men interceding with the Lord on behalf of the rich, increase their riches; and the rich, again, aiding the poor in their necessities, satisfy their souls. Both, therefore, are partners in the righteous work. He who does these things shall not be deserted by God, but shall be enrolled in the books of the living. Blessed are they who have riches, and who understand that they are from the Lord. [For they who are of that mind will be able to do some good.]"

SIMILITUDE THIRD

AS IN WINTER GREEN TREES CANNOT BE DISTINGUISHED FROM WITHERED, SO IN THIS WORLD NEITHER CAN THE JUST FROM THE UNJUST

He showed me many trees having no leaves, but withered, as it seemed to me; for all were alike. And he said to me, "Do you see those trees?" "I see, sir," I replied, "that all are alike, and withered." He answered me, and said, "These trees which you see are those who dwell in this world." "Why, then, sir," I said, "are they withered, as it were, and alike?" "Because," he said, "neither are the righteous manifest in this life, nor sinners, but they are alike; for this life is a winter to the righteous, and they do not manifest themselves, because they dwell with sinners: for as in winter trees that have cast their leaves are alike, and it is not seen which are dead and which are living, so in this world neither do the righteous show themselves, nor sinners, but all are alike one to another."

SIMILITUDE FOURTH

AS IN SUMMER LIVING TREES ARE DISTINGUISHED FROM WITHERED BY FRUIT AND LIVING LEAVES, SO IN THE WORLD TO COME THE JUST DIFFER FROM THE UNJUST IN HAPPINESS

He showed me again many trees, some budding, and others withered. And he said to me, "Do you see these trees?" "I see, sir," I replied, "some putting forth buds, and others withered." "Those," he said, "which are budding are the righteous who are to live in the world to come; for the coming world is the summer of the righteous, but the winter of sinners. When, therefore, the mercy of the Lord shines forth, then shall they be made manifest who are the servants of God, and all men shall be made manifest. For as in summer the fruits of each individual tree appear, and it is ascertained of what sort they are, so also the fruits of the righteous shall be manifest, and all who have been fruitful in that world shall be made known. But the heathen and sinners, like the withered trees which you saw, will be found to be those who have been withered and unfruitful in that world, and shall be burnt as wood, and [so] made manifest, because their actions were evil during their lives. For the sinners shall be consumed because they sinned and did not repent, and the heathen shall be burned because they knew not Him who created them. Do you therefore bear fruit, that in that summer your fruit may be known. And refrain from much business, and you will never sin: for they who are occupied with much business commit also many sins, being distracted about their affairs, and not at all serving their Lord. How, then," he continued, "can such a one ask and obtain anything from the Lord, if he serve Him not? They who serve Him shall obtain their requests, but they who serve Him not shall receive nothing. And in the performance even of a single action a man can serve the Lord; for his mind will not be perverted from the Lord, but he will serve Him, having a pure mind. If, therefore, you do these things, you shall be able to bear fruit for the life to come. And every one who will do these things shall bear fruit."

SIMILITUDE FIFTH

OF TRUE FASTING AND ITS REWARD: ALSO OF PURITY OF BODY

CHAP. I

While fasting and sitting on a certain mountain, and giving thanks to the Lord for all His dealings with me, I see the Shepherd sitting down beside me, and saying, "Why have you come hither [so] early in the morning?" "Because, sir," I answered, "I have a station." "What is a station?" he asked. "I am fasting, sir," I replied. "What is this fasting," he continued, "which you are observing?" "As I have been accustomed, sir," I reply, "so I fast." "You do not know," he says, "how to fast unto the Lord: this useless fasting which you observe to Him is of no value." "Why, sir," I answered, "do you say this?" "I say to you," he continued, "that the fasting which you think you observe is not a fasting. But I will teach you what is a full and acceptable fasting to the Lord. Listen," he continued: "God does not desire such an empty fasting. For fasting to God in this way you will do nothing for a righteous life; but offer to God a fasting of the following kind: Do no evil in your life, and serve the Lord with a pure heart: keep His commandments, walking in His precepts, and let no evil desire arise in your heart; and believe in God. If you do these things, and fear Him, and abstain from every evil thing, you will live unto God; and if you do these things, you will keep a great fast, and one acceptable before God."

CHAP. II

"Hear the similitude which I am about to narrate to you relative to fasting. A certain man had a field and many slaves, and he planted a certain part of the field with a vineyard, and selecting a faithful and beloved and much valued slave, he called him to him, and said, Take this vineyard which I have planted, and stake it until I come, and do nothing else to the vineyard; and attend to this order of mine, and you shall receive your freedom from me.' And the master of the slave departed to a foreign country. And when he was gone, the slave took and staked the vineyard; and when he had finished the staking of the vines, he saw that the vineyard was full of weeds. He then reflected, saying, I have kept this order of my master: I will dig up the rest of this vineyard, and it will be more beautiful when dug up; and being free of weeds, it will yield more fruit, not being choked by them.' He took, therefore, and dug up the vineyard, and rooted out all the weeds that were in it. And that vineyard became very beautiful and fruitful, having no weeds to choke it. And after a certain time the master of the slave and of the field returned, and entered into the vineyard. And seeing that the vines were suitably supported on stakes, and the ground, moreover, dug up, and all the weeds rooted out, and the vines fruitful, he was greatly pleased with the work of his slave. And calling his beloved son who was his heir, and his friends who were his councillors, he told them what orders he had given his slave, and what he had found performed. And they rejoiced along with the slave at the testimony which his master bore to him. And he said to them, I promised this slave freedom if he obeyed the command which I gave him; and he has kept my command, and done besides a good work to the vineyard, and has pleased me exceedingly. In return, therefore, for the work which he has done, I wish to make him co-heir with my son, because, having good thoughts, he did not neglect them, but carried them out.' With this resolution of the master his son and friends were well pleased, viz., that the slave should be co-heir with the son. After a few days the master made a feast, and sent to his slave many dishes from his table. And the slave receiving the dishes that were sent him from his master, took of them what was sufficient for himself, and distributed the rest among his fellow-slaves. And his fellow-slaves rejoiced to receive the dishes, and began to pray for him, that he might find still greater favour with his master for having so treated them. His master heard all these things that were done, and was again greatly pleased with his conduct. And the master again calling together his friends and his son, reported to them the slave's proceeding with regard to the dishes which he had sent him. And they were still more satisfied that the slave should become co-heir with his son."

CHAP. III

I said to him, "Sir, I do not see the meaning of these similitudes, nor am I able to comprehend them, unless you explain them to me." "I will explain them all to you," he said, "and whatever I shall mention in the course of our conversations I will show you. [Keep the commandments of the Lord, and you will be approved, and inscribed amongst the number of those who observe His commands.] And if you do any good beyond what is commanded by God, you will gain for yourself more abundant glory, and will be more honoured by God than you would otherwise be. If, therefore, in keeping the commandments of God, you do, in addition, these services, you will have joy if you observe them according to my command." I said to him, "Sir, whatsoever you enjoin upon me I will observe, for I know that you are with me." "I will be with you," he replied, "because you have such a desire for doing good; and I will be with all those," he added, "who have such a desire. This fasting," he continued, "is very good, provided the commandments of the Lord be observed. Thus, then, shall you observe the fasting which you intend to keep. First of all, be on your guard against every evil word, and every evil desire, and purify your heart from all the vanities of this world. If you guard against these things, your fasting will be perfect. And you will do also as follows. Having fulfilled what is written, in the day on which you fast you will taste nothing but bread and water; and having reckoned up the price of the dishes of that day which you intended to have eaten, you will give it to a widow, or an orphan, or to some person in want, and thus you will exhibit humility of mind, so that he who has received benefit from your humility may fill his own soul, and pray for you to the Lord. If you observe fasting, as I have commanded you, your sacrifice will be acceptable to God, and this fasting will be written down; and the service thus performed is noble, and sacred, and acceptable to the Lord. These things, therefore, shall you thus observe with your children, and all your house, and in observing them you will be blessed; and as many as hear these words and observe them shall be blessed; and whatsoever they ask of the Lord they shall receive."

CHAP. IV

I prayed him much that he would explain to me the similitude of the field, and of the master of the vineyard, and of the slave who staked the vineyard, and of the sakes, and of the weeds that were plucked out of the vineyard, and of the son, and of the friends who were fellow-councillors, for I knew that all these things were a kind of parable. And he answered me, and said, "You are exceedingly persistent with your questions. You ought not," he continued, "to ask any questions at all; for if it is needful to explain anything, it will be made known to you." I said to him, "Sir, whatsoever you show me, and do not explain, I shall have seen to no purpose, not understanding its meaning. In like manner, also, if you speak parables to me, and do not unfold them, I shall have heard your words in vain." And he answered me again, saying, "Every one who is the servant of God, and has his Lord in his heart, asks of Him understanding, and receives it, and opens up every parable; and the words of the Lord become known to him which are spoken in parables. But those who are weak and slothful in prayer, hesitate to ask anything from the Lord; but the Lord is full of compassion, and gives without fail to all who ask Him. But you, having been strengthened by the holy Angel, and having obtained from Him such intercession, and not being slothful, why do not you ask of the Lord understanding, and receive it from Him?" I said to him, "Sir, having you with me, I am necessitated to ask questions of you, for you show me all things, and converse with me; but if I were to see or hear these things without you, I would then ask the Lord to explain them."

CHAP. V

"I said to you a little ago," he answered, "that you were cunning and obstinate in asking explanations of the parables; but since you are so persistent, I shall unfold to you the meaning of the similitudes of the field, and of all the others that follow, that you may make them known to every one. Hear now," he said, "and understand them. The field is this world; and the Lord of the field is He who created, and perfected, and strengthened all things; [and the son is the Holy Spirit;] and the slave is the Son of God; and the vines are this people, whom He Himself planted; and the stakes are the holy angels of the Lord, who keep His people together; and the weeds that were plucked out of the vineyard are the iniquities of God's servants; and the dishes which He sent Him from His table are the commandments which He gave His people through His Son; and the friends and fellow-councillors are the holy angels who were first created; and the Master's absence from home is the time that remains until His appearing." I said to him, "Sir, all these are great, and marvellous, and glorious things. Could I, therefore," I continued, "understand them? No, nor could any other man, even if exceedingly wise. Moreover," I added, "explain to me what I am about to ask you." "Say what you wish," he replied. "Why, sir," I asked, "is the Son of God in the parable in the form of a slave?"

CHAP. VI

"Hear," he answered: "the Son of God is not in the form of a slave, but in great power and might." "How so, sir?" I said; "I do not understand." "Because," he answered, "God planted the vineyard, that is to say, He created the people, and gave them to His Son; and the Son appointed His angels over them to keep them; and He Himself purged away their sins, having suffered many trials and undergone many labours, for no one is able to dig without labour and toil. He Himself, then, having purged away the sins of the people, showed them the paths of life by giving them the law which He received from His Father. [You see," he said, "that He is the Lord of the people, having received all authority from His Father.] And why the Lord took His Son as councillor, and the glorious angels, regarding the heirship of the slave, listen. The holy, pre-existent Spirit, that created every creature, God made to dwell in flesh, which He chose. This flesh, accordingly, in which the Holy Spirit dwelt, was nobly subject to that Spirit, walking religiously and chastely, in no respect defiling the Spirit; and accordingly, after living excellently and purely, and after labouring and co-operating with the Spirit, and having in everything acted vigorously and courageously along with the Holy Spirit, He assumed it as a partner with it. For this conduct of the flesh pleased Him, because it was not defiled on the earth while having the Holy Spirit. He took, therefore, as fellow-councillors His Son and the glorious angels, in order that this flesh, which had been subject to the body without a fault, might have some place of tabernacle, and that it might not appear that the reward [of its servitude had been lost], for the flesh that has been found without spot or defilement, in which the Holy Spirit dwelt, [will receive a reward]. You have now the explanation of this parable also."

CHAP. VII

"I rejoice, sir," I said, "to hear this explanation." "Hear," again he replied: "Keep this flesh pure and stainless, that the Spirit which inhabits it may bear witness to it, and your flesh may be justified. See that the thought never arise in your mind that this flesh of yours is corruptible, and you misuse it by any act of defilement. If you defile your flesh, you will also defile the Holy Spirit; and if you defile your flesh [and spirit], you will not live." "And if any one, sir," I said, "has been hitherto ignorant, before he heard these words, how can such a man be saved who has defiled his flesh?" "Respecting former sins of ignorance," he said, "God alone is able to heal them, for to Him belongs all power. [But be on your guard now, and the all-powerful and compassionate God will heal former transgressions], if for the time to come you defile not your body nor your spirit; for both are common, and cannot be defiled, the one without the other: keep both therefore pure, and you will live unto God."

SIMILITUDE SIXTH

OF THE TWO CLASSES OF VOLUPTUOUS MEN, AND OF THEIR DEATH, FALLING AWAY, AND THE DURATION OF THEIR PUNISHMENT

CHAP. I

Sitting in my house, and glorifying the Lord for all that I had seen, and reflecting on the commandments, that they are excellent, and powerful, and glorious, and able to save a man's soul, I said within myself, "I shall be blessed if I walk in these commandments, and every one who walks in them will be blessed." While I was saying these words to myself, I suddenly see him sitting beside me, and hear him thus speak: "Why are you in doubt about the commandments which I gave you? They are excellent: have no doubt about them at all, but put on faith in the Lord, and you will walk in them, for I will strengthen you in them. These commandments are beneficial to those who intend to repent: for if they do not walk in them, their repentance is in vain. You, therefore, who repent cast away the wickedness of this world which wears you out; and by putting on all the virtues of a holy life, you will be able to keep these commandments, and will no longer add to the number of your sins. Walk, therefore, in these commandments of mine, and you will live unto God. All these things have been spoken to you by me." And after he had uttered these words, he said to me, "Let us go into the fields, and I will show you the shepherds of the flocks." "Let us go, sir," I replied. And we came to a certain plain, and he showed me a young man, a shepherd, clothed in a suit of garments of a yellow colour: and he was herding very many sheep, and these sheep were feeding luxuriously, as it were, and riotously, and merrily skipping hither and thither. The shepherd himself was merry, because of his flock; and the appearance of the shepherd was joyous, and he was running about amongst his flock. [And other sheep I saw rioting and luxuriating in one place, but not, however, leaping about.]

CHAP. II

And he said to me, "Do you see this shepherd?" "I see him, sir," I said. "This," he answered, "is the angel of luxury and deceit: he wears out the souls of the servants of God, and perverts them from the truth, deceiving them with wicked desires, through which they will perish; for they forget the commandments of the living God, and walk in deceits and empty luxuries; and they are ruined by the angel, some being brought to death, others to corruption." I said to him, "Sir, I do not know the meaning of these words, to death, and to corruption.'" "Listen," he said. "The sheep which you saw merry and leaping about, are those which have torn themselves away from God for ever, and have delivered themselves over to luxuries and deceits [of this world. Among them there is no return to life through repentance, because they have added to their other sins, and blasphemed the name of the Lord. Such men therefore, are appointed unto death. And the sheep which you saw not leaping, but feeding in one place, are they who have delivered themselves over to luxury and deceit], but have committed no blasphemy against the Lord. These have been perverted from the truth: among them there is the hope of repentance, by which it is possible to live. Corruption, then, has a hope of a kind of renewal, but death has everlasting ruin." Again I went forward a little way, and he showed me a tall shepherd, somewhat savage in his appearance, clothed in a white goatskin, and having a wallet on his shoulders, and a very hard staff with branches, and a large whip. And he had a very sour look, so that I was afraid of him, so forbidding was his aspect. This shepherd, accordingly, was receiving the sheep from the young shepherd, those, viz., that were rioting and luxuriating, but not leaping; and he cast them into a precipitous place, full of thistles and thorns, so that it was impossible to extricate the sheep from the thorns and thistles; but they were completely entangled amongst them. These, accordingly, thus entangled, pastured amongst the thorns and thistles, and were exceedingly miserable, being beaten by him; and he drove them hither and thither, and gave them no rest; and, altogether, these sheep were in a wretched plight.

CHAP. III

Seeing them, therefore, so beaten and so badly used, I was grieved for them, because they were so tormented, and had no rest at all. And I said to the Shepherd who talked with me, "Sir, who is this shepherd, who is so pitiless and severe, and so completely devoid of compassion for these sheep?" "This," he replied, "is the angel of punishment; and he belongs to the just angels, and is appointed to punish. He accordingly takes those who wander away from God, and who have walked in the desires and deceits of this world, and chastises them as they deserve with terrible and diverse punishments." "I would know, sir," I said, "Of what nature are these diverse tortures and punishments?" "Hear," he said, "the various tortures and punishments. The tortures are such as occur during life. For some are punished with losses, others with want, others with sicknesses of various kinds, and others with all kinds of disorder and confusion; others are insulted by unworthy persons, and exposed to suffering in many other ways: for many, becoming unstable in their plans, try many things, and none of them at all succeed, and they say they are not prosperous in their undertakings; and it does not occur to their minds that they have done evil deeds, but they blame the Lord. When, therefore, they have been afflicted with all kinds of affliction, then are they delivered unto me for good training, and they are made strong in the faith of the Lord; and for the rest of the days of their life they are subject to the Lord with pure hearts, and are successful in all their undertakings, obtaining from the Lord everything they ask; and then they glorify the Lord, that they were delivered to me, and no longer suffer any evil."

CHAP. IV

I said to him, "Sir, explain this also to me." "What is it you ask?" he said. "Whether, sir," I continued, "they who indulge in luxury, and who are deceived, are tortured for the same period of time that they have indulged in luxury and deceit?" He said to me, "They are tortured in the same manner." ["They are tormented much less, sir," I replied;] "for those who are so luxurious and who forget God ought to be tortured seven-fold." He said to me "You are foolish, and do not understand the power of torment." "Why, sir," I said, "if I had understood it, I would not have asked you to show me." "Hear," he said, "the power of both. The time of luxury and deceit is one hour; but the hour of torment is equivalent to thirty days. If, accordingly, a man indulge in luxury for one day, and be deceived and be tortured for one day, the day of his torture is equivalent to a whole year. For all the days of luxury, therefore, there are as many years of torture to be undergone. You see, then," he continued, "that the time of luxury and deceit is very short, but that of punishment and torture long."

CHAP. V

"Still," I said, "I do not quite understand about the time of deceit, and luxury, and torture; explain it to me more clearly." He answered, and said to me, "Your folly is persistent; and you do not wish to purify your heart, and serve God. Have a care," he added, "lest the time be fulfilled, and you be found foolish. Hear now," he added, "as you desire, that you may understand these things. He who indulges in luxury, and is deceived for one day, and who does what he wishes, is clothed with much foolishness, and does not understand the act which he does until the morrow; for he forgets what he did the day before. For luxury and deceit have no memories, on account of the folly with which they are clothed; but when punishment and torture cleave to a man for one day, he is punished and tortured for a year; for punishment and torture have powerful memories. While tortured and punished, therefore, for a whole year, he remembers at last his luxury and deceit, and knows that on their account he suffers evil. Every man, therefore, who is luxurious and deceived is thus tormented, because, although having life, they have given themselves over to death." "What kinds of luxury, sir," I asked, "are hurtful?" "Every act of a man which he performs with pleasure," he replied, "is an act of luxury; for the sharp-tempered man, when gratifying his tendency, indulges in luxury; and the adulterer, and the drunkard, and the back-biter, and the liar, and the covetous man, and the thief, and he who does things like these, gratifies his peculiar propensity, and in so doing indulges in luxury. All these acts of luxury are hurtful to the servants of God. On account of these deceits, therefore, do they suffer, who are punished and tortured. And there are also acts of luxury which save men; for many who do good indulge in luxury, being carried away by their own pleasure: this luxury, however, is beneficial to the servants of God, and gains life for such a man; but the injurious acts of luxury before enumerated bring tortures and punishment upon them; and if they continue in them and do not repent, they bring death upon themselves."

SIMILITUDE SEVENTH

THEY WHO REPENT MUST BRING FORTH FRUITS WORTHY OF REPENTANCE

After a few days I saw him in the same plain where I had also seen the shepherds; and he said to me, "What do you wish with me?" I said to him, "Sir, that you would order the shepherd who punishes to depart out of my house, because he afflicts me exceedingly." "It is necessary," he replied, "that you be afflicted; for thus," he continued, "did the glorious angel command concerning you, as he wishes you to be tried." "What have I done which is so bad, sir," I replied, "that I should be delivered over to this angel?" "Listen," he said: "Your sins are many, but not so great as to require that you be delivered over to this angel; but your household has committed great iniquities and sins, and the glorious angel has been incensed at them on account of their deeds; and for this reason he commanded you to be afflicted for a certain time, that they also might repent, and purify themselves from every desire of this world. When, therefore, they repent and are purified, then the angel of punishment will depart." I said to him, "Sir, if they have done such things as to incense the glorious angel against them, yet what have I done?" He replied, "They cannot be afflicted at all, unless you, the head of the house, be afflicted: for when you are afflicted, of necessity they also suffer affliction; but if you are in comfort, they can feel no affliction." "Well, sir," I said, "they have repented with their whole heart." "I know, too," he answered, "that they have repented with their whole heart: do you think, however, that the sins of those who repent are remitted? Not altogether, but he who repents must torture his own soul, and be exceedingly humble in all his conduct, and be afflicted with many kinds of affliction; and if he endure the afflictions that come upon him, He who created all things, and endued them with power, will assuredly have compassion, and will heal him; and this will He do when He sees the heart of every penitent pure from every evil thing: and it is profitable for you and for your house to suffer affliction now. But why should I say much to you? You must be afflicted, as that angel of the Lord commanded who delivered you to me. And for this give thanks to the Lord, because He has deemed you worthy of showing you beforehand this affliction, that, knowing it before it comes, you may be able to bear it with courage." I said to him, "Sir, be thou with me, and I will be able to bear all affliction." "I will be with you," he said, "and I will ask the angel of punishment to afflict you more lightly; nevertheless, you will be afflicted for a little time, and again you will be re-established in your house. Only continue humble, and serve the Lord in all purity of heart, you and your children, and your house, and walk in my commands which I enjoin upon you, and your repentance will be deep and pure; and if you observe these things with your household, every affliction will depart from you. And affliction," he added, "will depart from all who walk in these my commandments."

SIMILITUDE EIGHTH

THE SINS OF THE ELECT AND OF THE PENITENT ARE OF MANY KINDS, BUT ALL WILL BE REWARDED ACCORDING TO THE MEASURE OF THEIR REPENTANCE AND GOOD WORKS

CHAP. I

He showed me a large willow tree overshadowing plains and mountains, and under the shade of this willow had assembled all those who were called by the name of the Lord. And a glorious angel of the Lord, who was very tall, was standing beside the willow, having a large pruning-knife, and he was cutting little twigs from the willow and distributing them among the people that were overshadowed by the willow; and the twigs which he gave them were small, about a cubit, as it were, in length. And after they had all received the twigs, the angel laid down the pruning-knife, and that tree was sound, as I had seen it at first. And I marvelled within myself, saying, "How is the tree sound, after so many branches have been cut off?" And the Shepherd said to me, "Do not be surprised if the tree remains sound after so many branches were lopped off; [but wait,] and when you shall have seen everything, then it will be explained to you what it means." The angel who had distributed the branches among the people again asked them from them, and in the order in which they had received them were they summoned to him, and each one of them returned his branch. And the angel of the Lord took and looked at them. From some he received the branches withered and moth-eaten; those who returned branches in that state the angel of the Lord ordered to stand apart. Others, again, returned them withered, but not moth-eaten; and these he ordered to stand apart. And others returned them half-withered, and these stood apart; and others returned their branches half-withered and having cracks in them, and these stood apart. [And others returned their branches green and having cracks in them; and these stood apart.] And others returned their branches, one-half withered and the other green; and these stood apart. And others brought their branches two-thirds green and the remaining third withered; and these stood apart. And others returned them two-thirds withered and one-third green; and these stood apart. And others returned their branches nearly all green, the smallest part only, the top, being withered, but they had cracks in them; and these stood apart. And of others very little was green, but the remaining parts withered; and these stood apart. And others came bringing their branches green, as they had received them from the angel. And the majority of the crowd returned branches of that kind, and with these the angel was exceedingly pleased; and these stood apart. [And others returned their branches green and having offshoots; and these stood apart, and with these the angel was exceedingly delighted.] And others returned their branches green and with offshoots, and the offshoots had some fruit, as it were; and those men whose branches were found to be of that kind were exceedingly joyful. And the angel was exultant because of them; and the Shepherd also rejoiced greatly because of them.

CHAP. II

And the angel of the Lord ordered crowns to be brought; and there were brought crowns, formed, as it were, of palms; and he crowned the men who had returned the branches which had offshoots and some fruit, and sent them away into the tower. And the others also he sent into the tower, those, namely, who had returned branches that were green and had offshoots but no fruit, having given them seals. And all who went into the tower had the same clothing—white as snow. And those who returned their branches green, as they had received them, he set free, giving them clothing and seals. Now after the angel had finished these things, he said to the Shepherd, "I am going away, and you will send these away within the walls, according as each one is worthy to have his dwelling. And examine their branches carefully, and so dismiss them; but examine them with care. See that no one escape you," he added; "and if any escape you, I will try them at the altar." Having said these words to the Shepherd, he departed. And after the angel had departed, the Shepherd said to me, "Let us take the branches of all these and plant them, and see if any of them will live." I said to him, "Sir, how can these withered branches live?" He answered, and said, "This tree is a willow, and of a kind that is very tenacious of life. If, therefore, the branches be planted, and receive a little moisture, many of them will live. And now let us try, and pour water upon them; and if any of them live I shall rejoice with them, and if they do not I at least will not be found neglectful." And the Shepherd bade me call them as each one was placed. And they came, rank by rank, and gave their branches to the Shepherd. And the Shepherd received the branches, and planted them in rows; and after he had planted them he poured much water upon them, so that the branches could not be seen for the water; and after the branches had drunk it in, he said to me, "Let us go, and return after a few days, and inspect all the branches; for He who created this tree wishes all those to live who received branches from it. And I also hope that the greater part of these branches which received moisture and drank of the water will live."

CHAP. III

I said to him, "Sir, explain to me what this tree means, for I am perplexed about it, because, after so many branches have been cut off, it continues sound, and nothing appears to have been cut away from it. By this, now, I am perplexed." "Listen," he said: "This great tree that casts its shadow over plains, and mountains, and all the earth, is the law of God that was given to the whole world; and this law is the Son of God, proclaimed to the ends of the earth; and the people who are under its shadow are they who have heard the proclamation, and have believed upon Him. And the great and glorious angel Michael is he who has authority over this people, and governs them; for this is he who gave them the law into the hearts of believers: he accordingly superintends them to whom he gave it, to see if they have kept the same. And you see the branches of each one, for the branches are the law. You see, accordingly, many branches that have been rendered useless, and you will know them all—those who have not kept the law; and you will see the dwelling of each one." I said to him, "Sir, why did he dismiss some into the tower, and leave others to you?" "All," he answered, "who transgressed the law which they received from him, he left under my power for repentance; but all who have satisfied the law, and kept it, he retains under his own authority." "Who, then," I continued, "are they who were crowned, and who go to the tower?" "These are they who have suffered on account of the law; but the others, and they who returned their branches green, and with offshoots, but without fruit, are they who have been afflicted on account of the law, but who have not suffered nor denied their law; and they who returned their branches green as they had received them, are the venerable, and the just, and they who have walked carefully in a pure heart, and have kept the commandments of the Lord. And the rest you will know when I have examined those branches which have been planted and watered."

CHAP. IV

And after a few days we came to the place, and the Shepherd sat down in the angel's place, and I stood beside him. And he said to me, "Gird yourself with pure, undressed linen made of sackcloth;" and seeing me girded, and ready to minister to him, "Summon," he said, "the men to whom belong the branches that were planted, according to the order in which each one gave them in." So I went away to the plain, and summoned them all, and they all stood in their ranks. He said to them, "Let each one pull out his own branch, and bring it to me." The first to give in were those who had them withered and cut; and because they were found to be thus withered and cut, he commanded them to stand apart. And next they gave them in who had them withered, but not cut. And some of them gave in their branches green, and some withered and eaten as by a moth. Those that gave them in green, accordingly, he ordered to stand apart; and those who gave them in dry and cut, he ordered to stand along with the first. Next they gave them in who had them half-withered and cracked; and many of them gave them in green and without cracks; and some green and with offshoots and fruits upon the offshoots, such as they had who went, after being crowned, into the tower. And some handed them in withered and eaten, and some withered and uneaten; and some as they were, half-withered and cracked. And he commanded them each one to stand apart, some towards their own rows, and others apart from them.

CHAP. V

Then they gave in their branches who had them green, but cracked: all these gave them in green, and stood in their own row. And the Shepherd was pleased with these, because they were all changed, and had lost their cracks. And they also gave them in who had them half-green and half-withered: of some, accordingly, the branches were found completely green; of others, half-withered; of others, withered and eaten; of others, green, and having offshoots. All these were sent away, each to his own row. [Next they gave in who had them two parts green and one-third withered. Many of them gave them half-withered; and others withered and rotten; and others half-withered and cracked, and a few green. These all stood in their own row.] And they gave them in who had them green, but to a very slight extent withered and cracked. Of these, some gave them in green, and others green and with offshoots. And these also went away to their own row. Next they gave them who had a very small part green and the other parts withered. Of these the branches were found for the most part green and having offshoots, and fruit upon the offshoots, and others altogether green. With these branches the Shepherd was exceedingly pleased, because they were found in this state. And these went away, each to his own row.

CHAP. VI

After the Shepherd had examined the branches of them all, he said to me, "I told you that this tree was tenacious of life. You see," he continued, "how many repented and were saved." "I see, sir," I replied. "That you may behold," he added, "the great mercy of the Lord, that it is great and glorious, and that He has given His Spirit to those who are worthy of repentance." "Why then, sir," I said, "did not all these repent?" He answered, "To them whose heart He saw would become pure, and obedient to Him, He gave power to repent with the whole heart. But to them whose deceit and wickedness He perceived, and saw that they intended to repent hypocritically, He did not grant repentance, lest they should again profane His name." I said to him, "Sir, show me now, with respect to those who gave in the branches, of what sort they are, and their abode, in order that they hearing it who believed, and received the seal, and broke it, and did not keep it whole, may, on coming to a knowledge of their deeds, repent, and receive from you a seal, and may glorify the Lord because He had compassion upon them, and sent you to renew their spirits." "Listen," he said: "they whose branches were found withered and moth-eaten are the apostates and traitors of the Church, who have blasphemed the Lord in their sins, and have, moreover, been ashamed of the name of the Lord by which they were called. These, therefore, at the end were lost unto God. And you see that not a single one of them repented, although they heard the words which I spake to them, which I enjoined upon you. From such life departed. And they who gave them in withered and undecayed, these also were near to them; for they were hypocrites, and introducers of strange doctrines, and subverters of the servants of God, especially of those who had sinned, not allowing them to repent, but persuading them by foolish doctrines. These, accordingly, have a hope of repentance. And you see that many of them also have repented since I spake to them, and they will still repent. But all who will not repent have lost their lives; and as many of them as repented became good, and their dwelling was appointed within the first walls; and some of them ascended even into the tower. You see, then," he said, "that repentance involves life to sinners, but non-repentance death."

CHAP. VII

"And as many as gave in the branches half-withered and cracked, hear also about them. They whose branches were half-withered to the same extent are the wavering; for they neither live, nor are they dead. And they who have them half-withered and cracked are both waverers and slanderers, [railing against the absent,] and never at peace with one another, but always at variance. And yet to these also," he continued, "repentance is possible. You see," he said, "that some of them have repented, and there is still remaining in them," he continued, "a hope of repentance. And as many of them," he added, "as have repented, shall have their dwelling in the tower. And those of them who have been slower in repenting shall dwell within the walls. And as many as do not repent at all, but abide in their deeds, shall utterly perish. And they who gave in their branches green and cracked were always faithful and good, though emulous of each other about the foremost places, and about fame: now all these are foolish, in indulging in such a rivalry. Yet they also, being naturally good, on hearing my commandments, purified themselves, and soon repented. Their dwelling, accordingly, was in the tower. But if any one relapse into strife, he will be east out of the tower, and will lose his life. Life is the possession of all who keep the commandments of the Lord; but in the commandments there is no rivalry in regard to the first places, or glory of any kind, but in regard to patience and personal humility. Among such persons, then, is the life of the Lord, but amongst the quarrelsome and transgressors, death."

CHAP. VIII

"And they who gave in their branches half-green and half-withered, are those who are immersed in business, and do not cleave to the saints. For this reason, the one half of them is living, and the other half dead. Many, accordingly, who heard my commands repented, and those at least who repented had their dwelling in the tower. But some of them at last fell away: these, accordingly, have not repentance, for on account of their business they blasphemed the Lord, and denied Him. They therefore lost their lives through the wickedness which they committed. And many of them doubted. These still have repentance in their power, if they repent speedily; and their abode will be in the tower. But if they are slower in repenting, they will dwell within the walls; and if they do not repent, they too have lost their lives. And they who gave in their branches two-thirds withered and one-third green, are those who have denied [the Lord] in various ways. Many, however, repented, but some of them hesitated and were in doubt. These, then, have repentance within their reach, if they repent quickly, and do not remain in their pleasures; but if they abide in their deeds, these, too, work to themselves death."

CHAP. IX

"And they who returned their branches two-thirds withered and one-third green, are those that were faithful indeed; but after acquiring wealth, and becoming distinguished amongst the heathen, they clothed themselves with great pride, and became lofty-minded, and deserted the truth, and did not cleave to the righteous, but lived with the heathen, and this way of life became more agreeable to them. They did not, however, depart from God, but remained in the faith, although not working the works of faith. Many of them accordingly repented, and their dwelling was in the tower. And others continuing to live until the end with the heathen, and being corrupted by their vain glories, [departed from God, serving the works and deeds of the heathen.] These were reckoned with the heathen. But others of them hesitated, not hoping to be saved on account of the deeds which they had done; while others were in doubt, and caused divisions among themselves. To those, therefore, who were in doubt on account of their deeds, repentance is still open; but their repentance ought to be speedy, that their dwelling may be in the tower. And to those who do not repent, but abide in their pleasures, death is near."

CHAP. X

"And they who give in their branches green, but having the tips withered and cracked, these were always good, and faithful, and distinguished before God; but they sinned a very little through indulging small desires, and finding little faults with one another. But on hearing my words the greater part of them quickly repented, and their dwelling was upon the tower. Yet some of them were in doubt; and certain of them who were in doubt wrought greater dissension. Among these, therefore, is hope of repentance, because they were always good; and with difficulty will any one of them perish. And they who gave up their branches withered, but having a very small part green, are those who believed only, yet continue working the works of iniquity. They never, however, departed from God, but gladly bore His name, and joyfully received His servants into their houses. Having accordingly heard of this repentance, they unhesitatingly repented, and practice all virtue and righteousness; and some of them even [suffered, being willingly put to death], knowing their deeds which they had done. Of all these, therefore, the dwelling shall be in the tower."

CHAP. XI

And after he had finished the explanations of all the branches, he said to me, "Go and tell them to every one, that they may repent, and they shall live unto God. Because the Lord, having had compassion on all men, has sent me to give repentance, although some are not worthy of it on account of their works; but the Lord, being long-suffering, desires those who were called by His Son to be saved." I said to him, "Sir, I hope that all who have heard them will repent; for I am persuaded that each one, on coming to a knowledge of his own works, and fearing the Lord, will repent." He answered me, and said, "All who with their whole heart shall purify themselves from their wickedness before enumerated, and shall add no more to their sins, will receive healing from the Lord for their former transgressions, if they do not hesitate at these commandments; and they will live unto God. But do you walk in my commandments, and live." Having shown me these things, and spoken all these words, he said to me, "And the rest I will show you after a few days."

SIMILITUDE NINTH

THE GREAT MYSTERIES IN THE BUILDING OF THE MILITANT AND TRIUMPHANT CHURCH

CHAP. I

After I had written down the commandments and similitudes of the Shepherd, the angel of repentance, he came to me and said, "I wish to explain to you what the Holy Spirit that spake with you in the form of the Church showed you, for that Spirit is the Son of God. For, as you were somewhat weak in the flesh, it was not explained to you by the angel. When, however, you were strengthened by the Spirit, and your strength was increased, so that you were able to see the angel also, then accordingly was the building of the tower shown you by the Church. In a noble and solemn manner did you see everything as if shown you by a virgin; but now you see [them] through the same Spirit as if shown by an angel. You must, however, learn everything from me with greater accuracy. For I was sent for this purpose by the glorious angel to dwell in your house, that you might see all things with power, entertaining no fear, even as it was before." And he led me away into Arcadia, to a round hill; and he placed me on the top of the hill, and showed me a large plain, and round about the plain twelve mountains, all having different forms. The first was black as soot; and the second bare, without grass; and the third full of thorns and thistles; and the fourth with grass half-withered, the upper parts of the plants green, and the parts about the roots withered; and some of the grasses, when the sun scorched them, became withered. And the fifth mountain had green grass, and was ragged. And the sixth mountain was quite full of clefts, some small and others large; and the clefts were grassy, but the plants were not very vigorous, but rather, as it were, decayed. The seventh mountain, again, had cheerful pastures, and the whole mountain was blooming, and every kind of cattle and birds were feeding upon that mountain; and the more the cattle and the birds ate, the more the grass of that mountain flourished. And the eighth mountain was full of fountains, and every kind of the Lord's creatures drank of the fountains of that mountain. But the ninth mountain [had no water at all, and was wholly a desert, and had within it deadly serpents, which destroy men. And the tenth mountain] had very large trees, and was completely shaded, and under the shadow of the trees sheep lay resting and ruminating. And the eleventh mountain was very thickly wooded, and those trees were productive, being adorned with various sorts of fruits, so that any one seeing them would desire to eat of their fruits. The twelfth mountain, again, was wholly white, and its aspect was cheerful, and the mountain in itself was very beautiful.

CHAP. II

And in the middle of the plain he showed me a large white rock that had arisen out of the plain. And the rock was more lofty than the mountains, rectangular in shape, so as to be capable of containing the whole world: and that rock was old, having a gate cut out of it; and the cutting out of the gate seemed to me as if recently done. And the gate glittered to such a degree under the sunbeams, that I marvelled at the splendour of the gate; and round about the gate were standing twelve virgins. The four who stood at the corners seemed to me more distinguished than the others—they were all, however, distinguished—and they were standing at the four parts of the gate; two virgins between each part. And they were clothed with linen tunics, and gracefully girded, having their right shoulders exposed, as if about to bear some burden. Thus they stood ready; for they were exceedingly cheerful and eager. After I had seen these things, I marvelled in myself, because I was beholding great and glorious sights. And again I was perplexed about the virgins, because, although so delicate, they were standing courageously, as if about to carry the whole heavens. And the Shepherd said to me "Why are you reasoning in yourself, and perplexing your mind, and distressing yourself? for the things which you cannot understand, do not attempt to comprehend, as if you were wise; but ask the Lord, that you may receive understanding and know them. You cannot see what is behind you, but you see what is before. Whatever, then, you cannot see, let alone, and do not torment yourself about it: but what you see, make yourself master of it, and do not waste your labour about other things; and I will explain to you everything that I show you. Look therefore, on the things that remain."

CHAP. III

I saw six men come, tall, and distinguished, and similar in appearance, and they summoned a multitude of men. And they who came were also tall men, and handsome, and powerful; and the six men commanded them to build a tower above the rock. And great was the noise of those men who came to build the tower, as they ran hither and thither around the gate. And the virgins who stood around the gate told the men to hasten to build the tower. Now the virgins had spread out their hands, as if about to receive something from the men. And the six men commanded stones to ascend out of a certain pit, and to go to the building of the tower. And there went up ten shining rectangular stones, not hewn in a quarry. And the six men called the virgins, and bade them carry all the stones that were intended for the building, and to pass through the gate, and give them to the men who were about to build the tower. And the virgins put upon one another the ten first stones which had ascended from the pit, and carried them together, each stone by itself.

CHAP. IV

And as they stood together around the gate, those who seemed to be strong carried them, and they stooped down under the corners of the stone; and the others stooped down under the sides of the stones. And in this way they carried all the stones. And they carried them through the gate as they were commanded, and gave them to the men for the tower; and they took the stones and proceeded with the building. Now the tower was built upon the great rock, and above the gate. Those ten stones were prepared as the foundation for the building of the tower. And the rock and gate were the support of the whole of the tower. And after the ten stones other twenty [five] came up out of the pit, and these were fitted into the building of the tower, being carried by the virgins as before. And after these ascended thirty-five. And these in like manner were fitted into the tower. And after these other forty stones came up; and all these were cast into the building of the tower, [and there were four rows in the foundation of the tower,] and they ceased ascending from the pit. And the builders also ceased for a little. And again the six men commanded the multitude of the crowd to bear stones from the mountains for the building of the tower. They were accordingly brought from all the mountains of various colours, and being hewn by the men were given to the virgins; and the virgins carried them through the gate, and gave them for the building of the tower. And when the stones of various colours were placed in the building, they all became white alike, and lost their different colours. And certain stones were given by the men for the building, and these did not become shining; but as they were placed, such also were they found to remain: for they were not given by the virgins, nor carried through the gate. These stones, therefore, were not in keeping with the others in the building of the tower. And the six men, seeing these unsuitable stones in the building, commanded them to be taken away, and to be carried away down to their own place whence they had been taken; [and being removed one by one, they were laid aside; and] they say to the men who brought the stones, "Do not ye bring any stones at all for the building, but lay them down beside the tower, that the virgins may carry them through the gate, and may give them for the building. For unless," they said, "they be carried through the gate by the hands of the virgins, they cannot change their colours: do not toil, therefore," they said, "to no purpose."

CHAP. V

And on that day the building was finished, but the tower was not completed; for additional building was again about to be added, and there was a cessation in the building. And the six men commanded the builders all to withdraw a little distance, and to rest, but enjoined the virgins not to withdraw from the tower; and it seemed to me that the virgins had been left to guard the tower.

Now after all had withdrawn, and were resting themselves, I said to the Shepherd, "What is the reason that the building of the tower was not finished?" "The tower," he answered, "cannot be finished just yet, until the Lord of it come and examine the building, in order that, if any of the stones be found to be decayed, he may change them: for the tower is built according to his pleasure." "I would like to know, sir," I said, "what is the meaning of the building of this tower, and what the rock and gate, and the mountains, and the virgins mean, and the stones that ascended from the pit, and were not hewn, but came as they were to the building. Why, in the first place, were ten stones placed in the foundation, then twenty-five, then thirty-five, then forty? and I wish also to know about the stones that went to the building, and were again taken out and returned to their own place? On all these points put my mind at rest, sir, and explain them to me." "If you are not found to be curious about trifles," he replied, "you shall know everything. For after a few days [we shall come hither, and you will see the other things that happen to this tower, and will know accurately all the similitudes." After a few days] we came to the place where we sat down. And he said to me, "Let us go to the tower; for the master of the tower is coming to examine it." And we came to the tower, and there was no one at all near it, save the virgins only. And the Shepherd asked the virgins if perchance the master of the tower had come; and they replied that he was about to come to examine the building.

CHAP. VI

And, behold, after a little I see an array of many men coming, and in the midst of them one man of so remarkable a size as to overtop the tower. And the six men who had worked upon the building were with him, and many other honourable men were around him. And the virgins who kept the tower ran forward and kissed him, and began to walk near him around the tower. And that man examined the building carefully, feeling every stone separately; and holding a rod in his hand, he struck every stone in the building three times. And when he struck them, some of them became black as soot, and some appeared as if covered with scabs, and some cracked, and some mutilated, and some neither white nor black, and some rough and not in keeping with the other stones, and some having [very many] stains: such were the varieties of decayed stones that were found in the building. He ordered all these to be taken out of the tower, and to be laid down beside it, and other stones to be brought and put in their stead. [And the builders asked him from what mountain he wished them to be brought and put in their place.] And he did not command them to be brought from the mountains, [but he bade them be brought from a certain plain which was near at hand.] And the plain was dug up, and shining rectangular stones were found, and some also of a round shape; and all the stones which were in that plain were brought, and carried through the gate by the virgins. And the rectangular stones were hewn, and put in place of those that were taken away; but the rounded stones were not put into the building, because they were hard to hew, and appeared to yield slowly to the chisel; they were deposited, however, beside the tower, as if intended to be hewn and used in the building, for they were exceedingly brilliant.

CHAP. VII

The glorious man, the lord of the whole tower, having accordingly finished these alterations, called to him the Shepherd, and delivered to him all the stones that were lying beside the tower, that had been rejected from the building, and said to him, "Carefully clean all these stones, and put aside such for the building of the tower as may harmonize with the others; and those that do not, throw far away from the tower." [Having given these orders to the Shepherd, he departed from the tower], with all those with whom he had come. Now the virgins were standing around the tower, keeping it. I said again to the Shepherd, "Can these stones return to the building of the tower, after being rejected?" He answered me, and said, "Do you see these stones?" "I see them, sir," I replied. "The greater part of these stones," he said, "I will hew, and put into the building, and they will harmonize with the others." "How, sir," I said, "can they, after being cut all round about, fill up the same space?" He answered, "Those that shall be found small will be thrown into the middle of the building, and those that are larger will be placed on the outside, and they will hold them together." Having spoken these words, he said to me, "Let us go, and after two days let us come and clean these stones, and cast them into the building; for all things around the tower must be cleaned, lest the Master come suddenly and find the places about the tower dirty, and be displeased, and these stones be not returned for the building of the tower, and I also shall seem to be neglectful towards the Master." And after two days we came to the tower, and he said to me, "Let us examine all the stones, and ascertain those which may return to the building." I said to him, "Sir, let us examine them!"

CHAP. VIII

And beginning, we first examined the black stones. And such as they had been taken out of the building, were they found to remain; and the Shepherd ordered them to be removed out of the tower, and to be placed apart. Next he examined those that had scabs; and he took and hewed many of these, and commanded the virgins to take them up and cast them into the building. And the virgins lifted them up, and put them in the middle of the building of the tower. And the rest he ordered to be laid down beside the black ones; for these, too, were found to be black. He next examined those that had cracks; and he hewed many of these, and commanded them to be carried by the virgins to the building: and they were placed on the outside, because they were found to be sounder than the others; but the rest, on account of the multitude of the cracks, could not be hewn, and for this reason, therefore, they were rejected from the building of the tower. He next examined the chipped stones, and many amongst these were found to be black, and some to have great cracks. And these also he commanded to be laid down along with those which had been rejected. But the remainder, after being cleaned and hewn, he commanded to be placed in the building. And the virgins took them up, and fitted them into the middle of the building of the tower, for they were somewhat weak. He next examined those that were half white and half black, and many of them were found to be black. And he commanded these also to be taken away along with those which had been rejected. And the rest were all taken away by the virgins; for, being white, they were fitted by the virgins themselves into the building. And they were placed upon the outside, because they were found to be sound, so as to be able to support those which were placed in the middle, for no part of them at all was chipped. He next examined those that were rough and hard; and a few of them were rejected because they could not be hewn, as they were found exceedingly hard. But the rest of them were hewn, and carried by the virgins, and fitted into the middle of the building of the tower; for they were somewhat weak. He next examined those that had stains; and of these a very few were black, and were thrown aside with the others; but the greater part were found to be bright, and these were fitted by the virgins into the building, but on account of their strength were placed on the outside.

CHAP. IX

He next came to examine the white and rounded stones, and said to me, "What are we to do with these stones?" "How do I know, sir?" I replied. "Have you no intentions regarding them?" "Sir," I answered, "I am not acquainted with this art, neither am I a stone-cutter, nor can I tell." "Do you not see," he said, "that they are exceedingly round? and if I wish to make them rectangular, a large portion of them must be cut away; for some of them must of necessity be put into the building." "If therefore," I said, "they must, why do you torment yourself, and not at once choose for the building those which you prefer, and fit them into it?" He selected the larger ones among them, and the shining ones, and hewed them; and the virgins carried and fitted them into the outside parts of the building. And the rest which remained over were carried away, and laid down on the plain from which they were brought. They were not, however, rejected, "because," he said, "there remains yet a little addition to be built to the tower. And the lord of this tower wishes all the stones to be fitted into the building, because they are exceedingly bright." And twelve women were called, very beautiful in form, clothed in black, and with dishevelled hair. And these women seemed to me to be fierce. But the Shepherd commanded them to lift the stones that were rejected from the building, and to carry them away to the mountains from which they had been brought. And they were merry, and carried away all the stones, and put them in the place whence they had been taken. Now after all the stones were removed, and there was no longer a single one lying around the tower, he said, "Let us go round the tower and see, lest there be any defect in it." So I went round the tower along with him. And the Shepherd, seeing that the tower was beautifully built, rejoiced exceedingly; for the tower was built in such a way, that, on seeing it, I coveted the building of it, for it was constructed as if built of one stone, without a single joining. And the stone seemed as if hewn out of the rock; having to me the appearance of a monolith.

CHAP. X

And as I walked along with him, I was full of joy, beholding so many excellent things. And the Shepherd said to me, "Go and bring unslacked lime and fine-baked clay, that I may fill up the forms of the stones that were taken and thrown into the building; for everything about the tower must be smooth." And I did as he commanded me, and brought it to him. "Assist me," he said, "and the work will soon be finished." He accordingly filled up the forms of the stones that were returned to the building, and commanded the places around the tower to be swept and to be cleaned; and the virgins took brooms and swept the place, and carried all the dirt out of the tower, and brought water, and the ground around the tower became cheerful and very beautiful. Says the Shepherd to me, "Everything has been cleared away; if the lord of the tower come to inspect it, he can have no fault to find with us." Having spoken these words, he wished to depart; but I laid hold of him by the wallet, and began to adjure him by the Lord that he would explain what he had showed me. He said to me, "I must rest a little, and then I shall explain to you everything; wait for me here until I return." I said to him, "Sir, what can I do here alone?" "You are not alone," he said, "for these virgins are with you." "Give me in charge to them, then," I replied. The Shepherd called them to him, and said to them, "I entrust him to you until I come," and went away. And I was alone with the virgins; and they were rather merry, but were friendly to me, especially the four more distinguished of them.

CHAP. XI

The virgins said to me, "The Shepherd does not come here to-day." "What, then," said I, "am I to do?" They replied, "Wait for him until he comes; and if he comes he will converse with you, and if he does not come you will remain here with us until he does come." I said to them, "I will wait for him until it is late; and if he does not arrive, I will go away into the house, and come back early in the morning." And they answered and said to me, "You were entrusted to us; you cannot go away from us." "Where, then," I said, "am I to remain?" "You will sleep with us," they replied, "as a brother, and not as a husband: for you are our brother, and for the time to come we intend to abide with you, for we love you exceedingly!" But I was ashamed to remain with them. And she who seemed to be the first among them began to kiss me. [And the others seeing her kissing me, began also to kiss me], and to lead me round the tower, and to play with me. And I, too, became like a young man, and began to play with them: for some of them formed a chorus, and others danced, and others sang; and I, keeping silence, walked with them around the tower, and was merry with them. And when it grew late I wished to go into the house; and they would not let me, but detained me. So I remained with them during the night, and slept beside the tower. Now the virgins spread their linen tunics on the ground, and made me lie down in the midst of them; and they did nothing at all but pray; and I without ceasing prayed with them, and not less than they. And the virgins rejoiced because I thus prayed. And I remained there with the virgins until the next day at the second hour. Then the Shepherd returned, and said to the virgins, "Did you offer him any insult?" "Ask him," they said. I said to him, "Sir, I was delighted that I remained with them." "On what," he asked, "did you sup?" "I supped, sir," I replied, "on the words of the Lord the whole night." "Did they receive you well?" he inquired. "Yes, sir," I answered.

"Now," he said, "what do you wish to hear first?" "I wish to hear in the order," I said, "in which you showed me from the beginning. I beg of you, sir, that as I shall ask you, so also you will give me the explanation." "As you wish," he replied, "so also will I explain to you, and will conceal nothing at all from you."

CHAP. XII

"First of all, sir," I said, "explain this to me: What is the meaning of the rock and the gate?" "This rock," he answered, "and this gate are the Son of God." "How, sir?" I said; "the rock is old, and the gate is new." "Listen," he said, "and understand, O ignorant man. The Son of God is older than all His creatures, so that He was a fellow-councillor with the Father in His work of creation: for this reason is He old." "And why is the gate new, sir?" I said. "Because," he answered, "He became manifest in the last days of the dispensation: for this reason the gate was made new, that they who are to be saved by it might enter into the kingdom of God. You saw," he said, "that those stones which came in through the gate were used for the building of the tower, and that those which did not come, were again thrown back to their own place?" "I saw, sir," I replied. "In like manner," he continued, "no one shall enter into the kingdom of God unless he receive His holy name. For if you desire to enter into a city, and that city is surrounded by a wall, and has but one gate, can you enter into that city save through the gate which it has?" "Why, how can it be otherwise, sir?" I said. "If, then, you cannot enter into the city except through its gate, so, in like manner, a man cannot otherwise enter into the kingdom of God than by the name of His beloved Son. You saw," he added, "the multitude who were building the tower?" "I saw them, sir," I said. "Those," he said, "are all glorious angels, and by them accordingly is the Lord surrounded. And the gate is the Son of God. This is the one entrance to the Lord. In no other way, then, shall any one enter in to Him except through His Son. You saw," he continued, "the six men, and the tall and glorious man in the midst of them, who walked round the tower, and rejected the stones from the building?" "I saw him, sir," I answered. "The glorious man," he said, "is the Son of God, and those six glorious angels are those who support Him on the right hand and on the left. None of these glorious angels," he continued, "will enter in unto God apart from Him. Whosoever does not receive His name, shall not enter into the kingdom of God."

CHAP. XIII

"And the tower," I asked, "what does it mean?" "This tower," he replied, "is the Church." "And these virgins, who are they?" "They are holy spirits, and men cannot otherwise be found in the kingdom of God unless these have put their clothing upon them: for if you receive the name only, and do not receive from them the clothing, they are of no advantage to you. For these virgins are the powers of the Son of God. If you bear His name but possess not His power, it will be in vain that you bear His name. Those stones," he continued, "which you saw rejected bore His name, but did not put on the clothing of the virgins." "Of what nature is their clothing, sir?" I asked. "Their very names," he said, "are their clothing. Every one who bears the name of the Son of God, ought to bear the names also of these; for the Son Himself bears the names of these virgins. As many stones," he continued, "as you saw [come into the building of the tower through the hands] of these virgins, and remaining, have been clothed with their strength. For this reason you see that the tower became of one stone with the rock. So also they who have believed on the Lord through His Son, and are clothed with these spirits, shall become one spirit, one body, and the colour of their garments shall be one. And the dwelling of such as bear the names of the virgins is in the tower." "Those stones, sir, that were rejected," I inquired, "on what account were they rejected? for they passed through the gate, and were placed by the hands of the virgins in the building of the tower." "Since you take an interest in everything," he replied, "and examine minutely, hear about the stones that were rejected. These all," he said, "received the name of God, and they received also the strength of these virgins. Having received, then, these spirits, they were made strong, and were with the servants of God; and theirs was one spirit, and one body, and one clothing. For they were of the same mind, and wrought righteousness. After a certain time, however, they were persuaded by the women whom you saw clothed in black, and having their shoulders exposed and their hair dishevelled, and beautiful in appearance. Having seen these women, they desired to have them, and clothed themselves with their strength, and put off the strength of the virgins. These, accordingly, were rejected from the house of God, and were given over to these women. But they who were not deceived by the beauty of these women remained in the house of God. You have," he said, "the explanation of those who were rejected."

CHAP. XIV

"What, then, sir," I said, "if these men, being such as they are, repent and put away their desires after these women, and return again to the virgins, and walk in their strength and in their works, shall they not enter into the house of God?" "They shall enter in," he said, "if they put away the works of these women, and put on again the strength of the virgins, and walk in their works. For on this account was there a cessation in the building, in order that, if these repent, they may depart into the building of the tower. But if they do not repent, then others will come in their place, and these at the end will be cast out. For all these things I gave thanks to the Lord, because He had pity on all that call upon His name; and sent the angel of repentance to us who sinned against Him, and renewed our spirit; and when we were already destroyed, and had no hope of life, He restored us to newness of life." "Now, sir," I continued, "show me why the tower was not built upon the ground, but upon the rock and upon the gate." "Are you still," he said, "without sense and understanding?" "I must, sir," I said, "ask you of all things, because I am wholly unable to understand them; for all these things are great and glorious, and difficult for man to understand." "Listen," he said: "the name of the Son of God is great, and cannot be contained, and supports the whole world. If, then, the whole creation is supported by the Son of God, what think ye of those who are called by Him, and bear the name of the Son of God, and walk in His commandments? do you see what kind of persons He supports? Those who bear His name with their whole heart. He Himself, accordingly, became a foundation to them, and supports them with joy, because they are not ashamed to bear His name."

CHAP. XV

"Explain to me, sir," I said, "the names of these virgins, and of those women who were clothed in black raiment." "Hear," he said, "the names of the stronger virgins who stood at the corners. The first is Faith, the second Continence, the third Power, the fourth Patience. And the others standing in the midst of these have the following names: Simplicity, Innocence, Purity, Cheerfulness, Truth, Understanding, Harmony, Love. He who bears these names and that of the Son of God will be able to enter into the kingdom of God. Hear, also," he continued, "the names of the women who had the black garments; and of these four are stronger than the rest. The first is Unbelief, the second: Incontinence, the third Disobedience, the fourth Deceit. And their followers are called Sorrow, Wickedness, Wantonness, Anger, Falsehood, Folly, Backbiting, Hatred. The servant of God who bears these names shall see, indeed, the kingdom of God, but shall not enter into it." "And the stones, sir," I said, "which were taken out of the pit and fitted into the building: what are they?" "The first," he said, "the ten, viz., that were placed as a foundation, are the first generation, and the twenty-five the second generation, of righteous men; and the thirty-five are the prophets of God and His ministers; and the forty are the apostles and teachers of the preaching of the Son of God." "Why, then, sir," I asked, "did the virgins carry these stones also through the gate, and give them for the building of the tower?" "Because," he answered, "these were the first who bore these spirits, and they never departed from each other, neither the spirits from the men nor the men from the spirits, but the spirits remained with them until their falling asleep. And unless they had had these spirits with them, they would not have been of use for the building of this tower."

CHAP. XVI

"Explain to me a little further, sir," I said. "What is it that you desire?" he asked. "Why, sir," I said, "did these stones ascend out of the pit, and be applied to the building of the tower, after having borne these spirits?" "They were obliged," he answered, "to ascend through water in order that they might be made alive; for, unless they laid aside the deadness of their life, they could not in any other way enter into the kingdom of God. Accordingly, those also who fell asleep received the seal of the Son of God. For," he continued, "before a man bears the name of the Son of God he is dead; but when he receives the seal he lays aside his deadness, and obtains life. The seal, then, is the water: they descend into the water dead, and they arise alive. And to them, accordingly, was this seal preached, and they made use of it that they might enter into the kingdom of God." "Why, sir," I asked, "did the forty stones also ascend with them out of the pit, having already received the seal?" "Because," he said, "these apostles and teachers who preached the name of the Son of God, after falling asleep in the power and faith of the Son of God, preached it not only to those who were asleep, but themselves also gave them the seal of the preaching. Accordingly they descended with them into the water, and again ascended. [But these descended alive and rose up again alive; whereas they who had previously fallen asleep descended dead, but rose up again alive.] By these, then, were they quickened and made to know the name of the Son of God. For this reason also did they ascend with them, and were fitted along with them into the building of the tower, and, untouched by the chisel, were built in along with them. For they slept in righteousness and in great purity, but only they had not this seal. You have accordingly the explanation of these also."

CHAP. XVII

"I understand, sir," I replied. "Now, sir," I continued, "explain to me, with respect to the mountains, why their forms are various and diverse." "Listen," he said: "these mountains are the twelve tribes, which inhabit the whole world. The Son of God, accordingly, was preached unto them by the apostles." "But why are the mountains of various kinds, some having one form, and others another? Explain that to me, sir." "Listen," he answered: "these twelve tribes that inhabit the whole world are twelve nations. And they vary in prudence and understanding. As numerous, then, as are the varieties of the mountains which you saw, are also the diversities of mind and understanding among these nations. And I will explain to you the actions of each one." "First, sir," I said, "explain this: why, when the mountains are so diverse, their stones, when placed in the building, became one colour, shining like those also that had ascended out of the pit." "Because," he said, "all the nations that dwell under heaven were called by hearing and believing upon the name of the Son of God. Having, therefore, received the seal, they had one understanding and one mind; and their faith became one, and their love one, and with the name they bore also the spirits of the virgins. On this account the building of the tower became of one colour, bright as the sun. But after they had entered into the same place, and became one body, certain of these defiled themselves, and were expelled from the race of the righteous, and became again what they were before, or rather worse."

CHAP. XVIII

"How, sir," I said, "did they become worse, after having known God?" "He that does not know God," he answered, "and practices evil, receives a certain chastisement for his wickedness; but he that has known God, ought not any longer to do evil, but to do good. If, accordingly, when he ought to do good, he do evil, does not he appear to do greater evil than he who does not know God? For this reason, they who have not known God and do evil are condemned to death; but they who have known God, and have seen His mighty works, and still continue in evil, shall be chastised doubly, and shall die for ever. In this way, then, will the Church of God be purified. For as you saw the stones rejected from the tower, and delivered to the evil spirits, and cast out thence, so [they also shall be cast out, and] there shall be one body of the purified; as the tower also became, as it were, of one stone after its purification. In like manner also shall it be with the Church of God, after it has been purified, and has rejected the wicked, and the hypocrites, and the blasphemers, and the waverers, and those who commit wickedness of different kinds. After these have been cast away, the Church of God shall be one body, of one mind, of one understanding, of one faith, of one love. And then the Son of God will be exceeding glad, and shall rejoice over them, because He has received His people pure." "All these things, sir," I said, "are great and glorious."

"Moreover, sir," I said, "explain to me the power and the actions of each one of the mountains, that every soul, trusting in the Lord, and hearing it, may glorify His great, and marvellous, and glorious name." "Hear," he said, "the diversity of the mountains and of the twelve nations."

CHAP. XIX

"From the first mountain, which was black, they that believed are the following: apostates and blasphemers against the Lord, and betrayers of the servants of God. To these repentance is not open; but death lies before them, and on this account also are they black, for their race is a lawless one. And from the second mountain, which was bare, they who believed are the following: hypocrites, and teachers of wickedness. And these, accordingly, are like the former, not having any fruits of righteousness; for as their mountain was destitute of fruit, so also such men have a name indeed, but are empty of faith, and there is no fruit of truth in them. They indeed have repentance in their power, if they repent quickly; but if they are slow in so doing, they shall die along with the former." "Why, sir," I said, "have these repentance, but the former not? for their actions are nearly the same." "On this account," he said, "have these repentance, because they did not blaspheme their Lord, nor become betrayers of the servants of God; but on account of their desire of possessions they became hypocritical, and each one taught according to the desires of men that were sinners. But they will suffer a certain punishment; and repentance is before them, because they were not blasphemers or traitors."

CHAP. XX

"And from the third mountain, which had thorns and thistles, they who believed are the following. There are some of them rich, and others immersed in much business. The thistles are the rich, and the thorns are they who are immersed in much business. Those, [accordingly, who are entangled in many various kinds of business, do not] cleave to the servants of God, but wander away, being choked by their business transactions; and the rich cleave with difficulty to the servants of God, fearing lest these should ask something of them. Such persons, accordingly, shall have difficulty in entering the kingdom of God. For as it is disagreeable to walk among thistles with naked feet, so also it is hard for such to enter the kingdom of God. But to all these repentance, and that speedy, is open, in order that what they did not do in former times they may make up for in these days, and do some good, and they shall live unto God. But if they abide in their deeds, they shall be delivered to those women, who will put them to death."

CHAP. XXI

"And from the fourth mountain, which had much grass, the upper parts of the plants green, and the parts about the roots withered, and some also scorched by the sun, they who believed are the following: the doubtful, and they who have the Lord upon their lips, but have Him not in their heart. On this account their foundations are withered, and have no strength; and their words alone live, while their works are dead. Such persons are [neither alive nor] dead. They resemble, therefore, the waverers: for the wavering are neither withered nor green, being neither living nor dead. For as their blades, on seeing the sun, were withered, so also the wavering, when they hear of affliction, on account of their fear, worship idols, and are ashamed of the name of their Lord. Such, then, are neither alive nor dead. But these also may yet live, if they repent quickly; and if they do not repent, they are already delivered to the women, who take away their life."

CHAP. XXII

"And from the fifth mountain, which had green grass, and was rugged, they who believed are the following: believers, indeed, but slow to learn, and obstinate, and pleasing themselves, wishing to know everything, and knowing nothing at all. On account of this obstinacy of theirs, understanding departed from them, and foolish senselessness entered into them. And they praise themselves as having wisdom, and desire to become teachers, although destitute of sense. On account, therefore, of this loftiness of mind, many became vain, exalting themselves: for self-will and empty confidence is a great demon. Of these, accordingly, many were rejected, but some repented and believed, and subjected themselves to those that had understanding, knowing their own foolishness. And to the rest of this class repentance is open; for they were not wicked, but rather foolish, and without understanding. If these therefore repent, they will live unto God; but if they do not repent, they shall have their dwelling with the women who wrought wickedness among them."

CHAP. XXIII

"And those from the sixth mountain, which had clefts large and small, and decayed grass in the clefts, who believed, were the following: they who occupy the small clefts are those who bring charges against one another, and by reason of their slanders have decayed in the faith. Many of them, however, repented; and the rest also will repent when they hear my commandments, for their slanders are small, and they will quickly repent. But they who occupy the large clefts are persistent in their slanders, and vindictive in their anger against each other. These, therefore, were thrown away from the tower, and rejected from having a part in its building. Such persons, accordingly, shall have difficulty in living. If our God and Lord, who rules over all things, and has power over all His creation, does not remember evil against those who confess their sins, but is merciful, does man, who is corruptible and full of sins, remember evil against a fellow-man, as if he were able to destroy or to save him? I, the angel of repentance, say unto you, As many of you as are of this way of thinking, lay it aside, and repent, and the Lord will heal your former sins, if you purify yourselves from this demon; but if not, you will be delivered over to him for death."

CHAP. XXIV

"And those who believed from the seventh mountain, on which the grass was green and flourishing, and the whole of the mountain fertile, and every kind of cattle and the fowls of heaven were feeding on the grass on this mountain, and the grass on which they pastured became more abundant, were the following: they were always simple, and harmless, and blessed, bringing no charges against one another, but always rejoicing greatly because of the servants of God, and being clothed with the holy spirit of these virgins, and always having pity on every man, and giving aid from their own labour to every man, without reproach and without hesitation. The Lord, therefore, seeing their simplicity and all their meekness, multiplied them amid the labours of their hands, and gave them grace in all their doings. And I, the angel of repentance, say to you who are such, Continue to be such as these, and your seed will never be blotted out; for the Lord has made trial of you, and inscribed you in the number of us, and the whole of your seed will dwell with the Son of God; for ye have received of His Spirit."

CHAP. XXV

"And they who believed from the eighth mountain, where were the many fountains, and where all the creatures of God drank of the fountains, were the following: apostles, and teachers, who preached to the whole world, and who taught solemnly and purely the word of the Lord, and did not at all fall into evil desires, but walked always in righteousness and truth, according as they had received the Holy Spirit. Such persons, therefore, shall enter in with the angels."

CHAP. XXVI

"And they who believed from the ninth mountain, which was deserted, and had in it creeping things and wild beasts which destroy men, were the following: they who had the stains as servants, who discharged their duty ill, and who plundered widows and orphans of their livelihood, and gained possessions for themselves from the ministry, which they had received. If, therefore, they remain under the dominion of the same desire, they are dead, and there is no hope of life for them; but if they repent, and finish their ministry in a holy manner, they shall be able to live. And they who were covered with scabs are those who have denied their Lord, and have not returned to Him again; but becoming withered and desert-like, and not cleaving to the servants of God, but living in solitude, they destroy their own souls. For as a vine, when left within an enclosure, and meeting with neglect, is destroyed, and is made desolate by the weeds, and in time grows wild, and is no longer of any use to its master, so also are such men as have given themselves up, and become useless to their Lord, from having contracted savage habits. These men, therefore, have repentance in their power, unless they are found to have denied from the heart; but if any one is found to have denied from the heart, I do not know if he may live. And I say this not for these present days, in order that any one who has denied may obtain repentance, for it is impossible for him to be saved who now intends to deny his Lord; but to those who denied Him long ago, repentance seems to be possible. If, therefore, any one intends to repent, let him do so quickly, before the tower is completed; for if not, he will be utterly destroyed by the women. And the chipped stones are the deceitful and the slanderers; and the wild beasts which you saw on the ninth mountain, are the same. For as wild beasts destroy and kill a man by their poison, so also do the words of such men destroy and ruin a man. These, accordingly, are mutilated in their faith, on account of the deeds which they have done in themselves; yet some repented, and were saved. And the rest, who are of such a character, can be saved if they repent; but if they do not repent, they will perish with those women, whose strength they have assumed."

CHAP. XXVII

"And from the tenth mountain, where were trees which overshadowed certain sheep, they who believed were the following: bishops given to hospitality, who always gladly received into their houses the servants of God, without dissimulation. And the bishops never failed to protect, by their service, the widows, and those who were in want, and always maintained a holy conversation. All these, accordingly, shall be protected by the Lord for ever. They who do these things are honourable before God, and their place is already with the angels, if they remain to the end serving God."

CHAP. XXVIII

"And from the eleventh mountain, where were trees full of fruits, adorned with fruits of various kinds, they who believed were the following: they who suffered for the name of the Son of God, and who also suffered cheerfully with their whole heart, and laid down their lives." "Why, then, sir," I said, "do all these trees bear fruit, and some of them fairer than the rest?" "Listen," he said: "all who once suffered for the name of the Lord are honourable before God; and of all these the sins were remitted, because they suffered for the name of the Son of God. And why their fruits are of various kinds, and some of them superior, listen. All," he continued, "who were brought before the authorities and were examined, and did not deny, but suffered cheerfully—these are held in greater honour with God, and of these the fruit is superior; but all who were cowards, and in doubt, and who reasoned in their hearts whether they would deny or confess, and yet suffered, of these the fruit is less, because that suggestion came into their hearts; for that suggestion—that a servant should deny his Lord—is evil. Have a care, therefore, ye who are planning such things, lest that suggestion remain in your hearts, and ye perish unto God. And ye who suffer for His name ought to glorify God, because He deemed you worthy to bear

His name, that all your sins might be healed. [Therefore, rather deem yourselves happy], and think that ye have done a great thing, if any of you suffer on account of God. The Lord bestows upon you life, and ye do not understand, for your sins were heavy; but if you had not suffered for the name of the Lord, ye would have died to God on account of your sins. These things I say to you who are hesitating about denying or confessing: acknowledge that ye have the Lord, lest, denying Him, ye be delivered up to prison. If the heathen chastise their slaves, when one of them denies his master, what, think ye, will your Lord do, who has authority over all men? Put away these counsels out of your hearts, that you may live continually unto God."

CHAP. XXIX

"And they who believed from the twelfth mountain, which was white, are the following: they are as infant children, in whose hearts no evil originates; nor did they know what wickedness is, but always remained as children. Such accordingly, without doubt, dwell in the kingdom of God, because they defiled in nothing the commandments of God; but they remained like children all the days of their life in the same mind. All of you, then, who shall remain stedfast, and be as children, without doing evil, will be more honoured than all who have been previously mentioned; for all infants are honourable before God, and are the first persons with Him. Blessed, then, are ye who put away wickedness from yourselves, and put on innocence. As the first of all will you live unto God."

After he had finished the similitudes of the mountains, I said to him, "Sir, explain to me now about the stones that were taken out of the plain, and put into the building instead of the stones that were taken out of the tower; and about the round stones that were put into the building; and those that still remain round."

CHAP. XXX

"Hear," he answered, "about all these also. The stones taken out of the plain and put into the building of the tower instead of those that were rejected, are the roots of this white mountain. When, therefore, they who believed from the white mountain were all found guileless, the Lord of the tower commanded those from the roots of this mountain to be cast into the building of the tower; for he knew that if these stones were to go to the building of the tower, they would remain bright, and not one of them become black. But if he had so resolved with respect to the other mountains, it would have been necessary for him to visit that tower again, and to cleanse it. Now all these persons were found white who believed, and who will yet believe, for they are of the same race. This is a happy race, because it is innocent. Hear now, further, about these round and shining stones. All these also are from the white mountain. Hear, moreover, why they were found round: because their riches had obscured and darkened them a little from the truth, although they never departed from God; nor did any evil word proceed out of their mouth, but all justice, virtue, and truth. When the Lord, therefore, saw the mind of these persons, that they were born good, and could be good, He ordered their riches to be cut down, not to be taken away for ever, that they might be able to do some good with what was left them; and they will live unto God, because they are of a good race. Therefore were they rounded a little by the chisel, and put in the building of the tower.

CHAP. XXXI

"But the other round stones, which had not yet been adapted to the building of the tower, and had not yet received the seal, were for this reason put back into their place, because they are exceedingly round. Now this age must be cut down in these things, and in the vanities of their riches, and then they will meet in the kingdom of God; for they must of necessity enter into the kingdom of God, because the Lord has blessed this innocent race. Of this race, therefore, no one will perish; for although any of them be tempted by the most wicked devil, and commit sin, he will quickly return to his Lord. I deem you happy, I, who am the messenger of repentance, whoever of you are innocent as children, because your part is good, and honourable before God. Moreover, I say to you all, who have received the seal of the Son of God, be clothed with simplicity, and be not mindful of offences, nor remain in wickedness. Lay aside, therefore, the recollection of your offences and bitternesses, and you will be formed in one spirit. And heal and take away from you those wicked schisms, that if the Lord of the flocks come, He may rejoice concerning you. And He will rejoice, if He find all things sound, and none of you shall perish. But if He find any one of these sheep strayed, woe to the shepherds! And if the shepherds themselves have strayed, what answer will they give Him for their flocks? Will they perchance say that they were harassed by their flocks? They will not be believed, for the thing is incredible that a shepherd could suffer from his flock; rather will he be punished on account of his falsehood. And I myself am a shepherd, and I am under a most stringent necessity of rendering an account of you.

CHAP. XXXII

"Heal yourselves, therefore, while the tower is still building. The Lord dwells in men that love peace, because He loved peace; but from the contentious and the utterly wicked He is far distant. Restore to Him, therefore, a spirit sound as ye received it. For when you have given to a fuller a new garment, and desire to receive it back entire at the end, if, then, the fuller return you a torn garment, will you take it from him, and not rather be angry, and abuse him, saying, I gave you a garment that was entire: why have you rent it, and made it useless, so that it can be of no use on account of the rent which you have made in it?' Would you not say all this to the fuller about the rent which you found in your garment? If, therefore, you grieve about your garment, and complain because you have not received it entire, what do you think the Lord will do to you, who gave you a sound spirit, which you have rendered altogether useless, so that it can be of no service to its possessor? for its use began to be unprofitable, seeing it was corrupted by you. Will not the Lord, therefore, because of this conduct of yours regarding His Spirit, act in the same way, and deliver you over to death? Assuredly, I say, he will do the same to all those whom He shall find retaining a recollection of offences. Do not trample His mercy under foot, He says, but rather honour Him, because He is so patient with your sins, and is not as ye are. Repent, for it is useful to you."

CHAP. XXXIII

"All these things which are written above, I, the Shepherd, the messenger of repentance, have showed and spoken to the servants of God. If therefore ye believe, and listen to my words, and walk in them, and amend your ways, you shall have it in your power to live: but if you remain in wickedness, and in the recollection of offences, no sinner of that class will live unto God. All these words which I had to say have been spoken unto you."

The Shepherd said to me, "Have you asked me everything?" And I replied, "Yes, sir." "Why did you not ask me about the shape of the stones that were put into the building, that I might explain to you why we filled up the shapes?" And I said, "I forgot, sir." "Hear now, then," he said, "about this also. These are they who have now heard my commandments, and repented with their whole hearts. And when the Lord saw that their repentance was good and pure, and that they were able to remain in it, He ordered their former sins to be blotted out. For these shapes were their sins, and they were levelled down, that they might not appear."

SIMILITUDE TENTH

CONCERNING REPENTANCE AND ALMS-GIVING

CHAP. I

After I had fully written down this book, that messenger who had delivered me to the Shepherd came into the house in which I was, and sat down upon a couch, and the Shepherd stood on his right hand. He then called me, and spoke to me as follows: "I have delivered you and your house to the Shepherd, that you may be protected by him." "Yes, sir," I said. "If you wish, therefore, to be protected," he said, "from all annoyance, and from all harsh treatment, and to have success in every good work and word, and to possess all the virtues of righteousness, walk in these commandments which he has given you, and you will be able to subdue all wickedness. For if you keep those commandments, every desire and pleasure of the world will be subject to you, and success will attend you in every good work. Take unto yourself his experience and moderation, and say to all that he is in great honour and dignity with God, and that he is a president with great power, and mighty in his office. To him alone throughout the whole world is the power of repentance assigned. Does he seem to you to be powerful? But you despise his experience, and the moderation which he exercises towards you."

CHAP. II

I said to him, "Ask himself, sir, whether from the time that he has entered my house I have done anything improper, or have offended him in any respect." He answered, "I also know that you neither have done nor will do anything improper, and therefore I speak these words to you, that you may persevere. For he had a good report of you to me, and you will say these words to others, that they also who have either repented or will still repent may entertain the same feelings with you, and he may report well of these to me, and I to the Lord." And I said, "Sir, I make known to every man the great works of God: and I hope that all those who love them, and have sinned before, on hearing these words, may repent, and receive life again." "Continue, therefore, in this ministry, and finish it. And all who follow out his commands shall have life, and great honour with the Lord. But those who do not keep his commandments, flee from his life, and despise him. But he has his own honour with the Lord. All, therefore, who shall despise him, and not follow his commands, deliver themselves to death, and every one of them will be guilty of his own blood. But I enjoin you, that you obey his commands, and you will have a cure for your former sins."

CHAP. III

"Moreover, I sent you these virgins, that they may dwell with you. For I saw that they were courteous to you. You will therefore have them as assistants, that you may be the better able to keep his commands: for it is impossible that these commandments can be observed without these virgins. I see, moreover, that they abide with you willingly; but I will also instruct them not to depart at all from your house: do you only keep your house pure, as they will delight to dwell in a pure abode. For they are pure, and chaste, and industrious, and have all influence with the Lord. Therefore, if they find your house to be pure, they will remain with you; but if any defilement, even a little, befall it, they will immediately withdraw from your house. For these virgins do not at all like any defilement." I said to him, "I hope, sir, that I will please them, so that they may always be willing to inhabit my house. And as he to whom you entrusted me has no complaint against me, so neither will they have." He said to the Shepherd, "I see that the servant of God wishes to live, and to keep these commandments, and will place these virgins in a pure habitation." When he had spoken these words he again delivered me to the Shepherd, and called those virgins, and said to them, "Since I see that you are willing to dwell in his house, I commend him and his house to you, asking that you withdraw not at all from it." And the virgins heard these words with pleasure.

CHAP. IV

The angel then said to me, "Conduct yourself manfully in this service, and make known to every one the great things of God, and you will have favour in this ministry. Whoever, therefore, shall walk in these commandments, shall have life, and will be happy in his life; but whosoever shall neglect them shall not have life, and will be unhappy in this life. Enjoin all, who are able to act rightly, not to cease well-doing; for, to practice good works is useful to them. And I say that every man ought to be saved from inconveniences. For both he who is in want, and he who suffers inconveniences in his daily life, is in great torture and necessity. Whoever, therefore, rescues a soul of this kind from necessity, will gain for himself great joy. For he who is harassed by inconveniences of this kind, suffers equal torture with him who is in chains. Moreover many, on account of calamities of this sort, when they could not endure them, hasten their own deaths. Whoever, then, knows a calamity of this kind afflicting a man, and does not save him, commits a great sin, and becomes guilty of his blood. Do good works, therefore, ye who have received good from the Lord; lest, while ye delay to do them, the building of the tower be finished, and you be rejected from the edifice: there is now no other tower a-building. For on your account was the work of building suspended. Unless, then, you make haste to do rightly, the tower will be completed, and you will be excluded."

After he had spoken with me he rose up from the couch, and taking the Shepherd and the virgins, he departed. But he said to me that he would send back the Shepherd and the virgins to my dwelling. Amen.

THE WORKS OF THE SHEPHERD OF HERMAS

THE SHEPHERD OF HERMAS

AVAILABLE IN PAPERBACK.

TRANSLATED BY THE REV. F. CROMBIE, M.A.

THE WORKS OF THE SHEPHERD OF HERMAS

Introductory Note

[AD 160.] The fragment known as the "Muratorian Canon" is the historic ground for the date I give to this author. I desired to prefix The Shepherd to the writings of Irenæus, but the limits of the volume would not permit. The Shepherd attracted my attention, even in early youth, as a specimen of primitive romance; but of course it disappointed me, and excited repugnance. As to its form, it is even now distasteful. But more and more, as I have studied it, and cleared up the difficulties which surround it, and the questions it has started, it has become to me a most interesting and suggestive relic of the primitive age. Dr. Bunsen calls it "a good but dull novel," and reminds us of a saying of Niebuhr (Bunsen's master), that "he pitied the Athenian Christians for being obliged to hear it read in their assemblies." A very natural, but a truly superficial, thought, as I trust I shall be able to show.

At first sight, Hermas might seem to have little in common with Irenæus; and, on many accounts, it would be preferable to pair him with Barnabas. But I feel sure that chronology forbids, and that the age of Irenæus, and of the martyrs of Lyons and Vienne, is the period which called for this work, and which accounts for its popularity and its diffusion among the churches. Its pacific spirit in dealing with a rising heresy, which at first was a puzzle to the Latins, which Pius was disposed to meet by this gentle antidote, with which Eleutherus, in the spirit of a pacificator, tampered to his own hurt, and by which Victor was temporarily compromised, met precisely what the case seemed to demand in the judgment of Western Christians. They could not foresee the results of Montanism: it was not yet a defined heresy. And even the wise prudence of Irenæus shows anxiety not too hastily to denounce it; "seeing," as Eusebius affirms, "there were many other wonderful powers of divine grace yet exhibited, even at that time, in different churches."

Bunsen pronounces magisterially on the Muratorian fragment as an ill-translated excerpt from Hegesippus, written about AD 165. This date may be inaccurate, but the evidence is that of a contemporary on which we may rely. "Very recently," he says, "in our own times, in the city of Rome, Hermas compiled The Shepherd; his brother, Bishop Pius, then sitting in the cathedra of the Roman Church." With the period thus assigned, the internal evidence agrees. It accounts for the anti-Montanism of the whole allegory, and not less for the choice of this non-controversial form of antidote. Montanism is not named; but it is opposed by a reminder of better "prophesyings," and by setting the pure spirit of the apostolic age over against the frenzied and pharisaical pretensions of the fanatics. The pacific policy at first adopted by the Roman bishops, dictated, no doubt, this effort of Hermas to produce such a refutation as his brother might commend to the churches.

Let me present, in outline, the views which seem to me necessary to a good understanding of the work; and as I am so unfortunate as to differ with the Edinburgh editors, who are entitled, primâ facie, to be supposed correct, I shall venture to apologize for my own conceptions, by a few notes and elucidations.

As Eusebius informs us, the charismata were not extinct in the churches when the Phrygian imitations began to puzzle the faithful. Bunsen considers its first propagators specimens of the clairvoyant art, and pointedly cites the manipulations they were said to practice (like persons playing on the harp), in proof of this. We must place ourselves in those times to comprehend the difficulties of early Christians in dealing with the counterfeit. "Try the spirits," said St. John; and St. Paul had said more expressly, "Quench not the Spirit; despise not prophesyings; prove all things," etc. This very expression suggests that there might often be something despicable in the form and manner of uttering what was excellent. To borrow a phrase of our days, "the human element" was painfully predominant at times, even among those who spoke by the Spirit. The smoke of personal infirmity discoloured genuine scintillations from hearts in which still smouldered the fire of Pentecostal gifts. The reticence of Irenæus is therefore not to be marvelled at. He cautioned Eleutherus no doubt, but probably felt, with him, that the rumours from Phrygia needed further examination. The prophetic gifts were said to be lodged in men and women austere as John the Baptist, and professing a mission to rebuke the carnal and self-indulgent degeneracy of a generation that knew not the apostles.

It would not be a very bold conjecture, that Hermas and his brother were elderly grandchildren of the original Hermas, the friend of St. Paul. The Shepherd, then, might be based upon personal recollections, and upon the traditions of a family which the spirit of prophecy had reproved, and who were monuments of its power. The book supplies us with evidences of the awakened conscience with which Hermas strove to "bless his household." But, be this as it may, this second Hermas, with his brother's approbation, undertakes to revive the memory of those primal days portrayed in the Epistle to Diognetus, when Christians, though sorrowful, were "always rejoicing." He compiles accordingly a non-metrical idyl; reproducing, no doubt, traditional specimens of those "prophesyings," on which St. Paul remarks. Hence we infer, that such outpourings as became the subject of apostolic censure, when they confused the order of the Corinthian Church, were, in their nobler examples, such "visions," "mandates" and "similitudes" as these; more or less human as to form, but, in their moral teachings, an impressive testimony against heathen oracles, and their obscene or blasphemous suggestions.

The permissive wisdom of the Spirit granting, while restraining, such manifestations, is seen in thus counterbalancing Sibylline and other ethnic utterances. (Acts xvi. 16–19.) With this in view, Hermas makes his compilation. He casts it into an innocent fiction, as Cowper wrote in the name of Alexander Selkirk, and introduces Hermas and Clement to identify the times which are idealized in his allegory. Very gently, but forcibly, therefore, he brings back the original Christians as antagonists of the Montanistic opinions; and so exclusively does this idea predominate in the whole work, as Tertullian's scornful comment implies, that one wonders to find Wake, with other very learned men, conceding that the Pauline Hermas was its actual author. Were it so, he must have been a prophet indeed. No doubt those of the ancients who knew nothing of the origin of the work, and accepted it as the production of the first Hermas, were greatly influenced by this idea. It seemed to them a true oracle from God, like those of the Apocalypse, though sadly inferior; preparing the Church for one of its great trials and perils, and fulfilling, as did the Revelation of St. John, that emphatic promise concerning the Spirit, "He shall show you things to come."

This view of the subject, moreover, explains historical facts which have been so unaccountable to many critics; such as the general credit it obtained, and that its influence was greater in the East than among Latins. But once commended to the Asiatic churches by Pius, as a useful instruction for the people, and a safeguard against the Phrygian excesses, it would easily become current wherever the Greek language prevailed. Very soon it would be popularly regarded as the work of the Pauline Hermas, and as embodying genuine prophesyings of the apostolic age. A qualified inspiration would thus be attributed to them, precisely such as the guarded language of Origen suggested afterwards: hence the deutero-canonical repute of the book, read, like the Apocrypha, for instruction and edification, but not cited to establish any doctrine as of the faith. It must be remembered, that, although the Roman Church was at first a Grecian colony, and largely composed of those Hellenistic Jews to whom St. Paul's arguments in his Epistle to the Romans were personally appropriate, yet in the West, generally, it was not so: hence the greater diffusion of The Shepherd written in Greek, through the Greek churches. There, too, the Montanists were a raging pestilence long before the West really felt the contagion through the influence of the brilliant Tertullian. These facts account for the history of the book, its early currency and credit in the Church. Nor must we fail to observe, that the tedious allegorizing of Hermas, though not acceptable to us, was by no means displeasing to Orientals. To this day, the common people, even with us, seem to be greatly taken with story-telling and "similitudes," especially when there is an interpreter to give them point and application.

After reading Irenæus Against Heresies, then, we may not inappropriately turn to this mild protest against the most desolating and lasting delusion of primitive times. Most bitterly this will be felt when we reach the great founder of "Latin Christianity," whose very ashes breathed contagion into the life of such as handled his relics with affection, save only those, who, like Cyprian, were gifted with a character as strong as his own. The genius of Tertullian inspired his very insanity with power, and, to the discipline of the Latin churches, he communicated something of the rigour of Montanism, with the natural re-actionary relaxation of morals in actual life. Of this, we shall learn enough when we come to read the fascinating pages of that splendid but infatuated author. Montanism itself, and the Encratite heresy which we are soon to consider in the melancholy case of Tatian, were re-actions from those abominations of the heathen with which Christians were daily forced to be conversant. These Fathers erred through a temptation in which Satan was "transformed as an angel of light." Let us the more admire the penetrating foresight, and the holy moderation, of Hermas. To our scornful age, indeed, glutted with reading of every sort, and alike over-cultivated and superficial, taking little time for thought, and almost as little for study, The Shepherd can furnish nothing attractive. He who brings nothing to it, gets nothing from it. But let the fastidious who desire at the same time to be competent judges, put themselves into the times of the Antonines, and make themselves, for the moment, Christians of that period, and they will awaken to a new world of thought. Let such go into the assemblies of the primitive faithful, in which it was evident that "not many wise men after the flesh, not many mighty, not many noble, were called." There they were, "as sheep appointed to be slain," "dying daily," and, like their blessed Master, "the scorn of men, and outcast of the people," as they gathered on the day of the Lord to "eat of that bread, and drink of that cup." After the manner of the synagogue, there came a moment when the "president" said, "Brethren, if ye have any word of exhortation for the people, say on." But the tongues were ceasing, as the apostle foretold; and they who professed to speak by the Spirit were beginning to be doubted. "Your fathers, where are they? and the prophets, do they live forever?" It was gratifying to the older men, and excited the curiosity of the young, when the reader stood up, and said, "Hear, then, the words of Hermas." Blessed were the simple folk, those "lambs among wolves," who hungered and thirsted after righteousness, and who eagerly drank in the pure and searching Scriptural morality of The Shepherd, and then went forth to "shine as lights in the world," in holy contrast with the gross darkness that surrounded them.

It has been objected, indeed, that the morals of Hermas have a legalizing tone. The same is said of St. James, and the Sermon on the Mount. Most unjustly and cruelly is this objection made to The Shepherd. Granted its language is not formulated after Augustine, as it could not be: its text is St. James, but, like St. James, harmonized always with St. Paul. Faith is always honoured in its primary place; and penitence, in its every evangelical aspect, is thoroughly defined. He exposes the emptiness of formal works, such as mere physical fastings, and the carnal observance of set times and days. That in one instance he favours "works of supererogation" is an entire mistake, made by reading into the words of Hermas a heresy of which he never dreamed. His whole teaching conflicts with such a thought. His orthodoxy in other respects, is sustained by such masters as Pearson and Bull. And then, the positive side of his teaching is a precious testimony to the godly living exacted of believers in the second century. How suitable to all times are the maxims he extracts from the New Law. How searching his exposure of the perils of lax family discipline, and of wealth unsanctified. What heavenly precepts of life he lays down for all estates of men. To the clergy, what rules he prescribes against ambition and detraction and worldly-mindedness. Surely such reproofs glorify the epoch, when they who had cast off, so recently, the lusts and passions of heathenism, were, as the general acceptance of this book must lead us to suppose, eager to be fed with "truth, severe in rugged fiction drest."

But the reader will now be eager to examine the following:

Introductory Notice of the Translator

The Pastor of Hermas was one of the most popular books, if not the most popular book, in the Christian Church during the second, third, and fourth centuries. It occupied a position analogous in some respects to that of Bunyan's Pilgrim's Progress in modern times; and critics have frequently compared the two works.

In ancient times two opinions prevailed in regard to the authorship. The most widely spread was, that the Pastor of Hermas was the production of the

Hermas mentioned in the Epistle to the Romans. Origen states this opinion distinctly, and it is repeated by Eusebius and Jerome.

Those who believed the apostolic Hermas to be the author, necessarily esteemed the book very highly; and there was much discussion as to whether it was inspired or not. The early writers are of opinion that it was really inspired. Irenæus quotes it as Scripture; Clemens Alexandrinus speaks of it as making its statements "divinely;" and Origen, though a few of his expressions are regarded by some as implying doubt, unquestionably gives it as his opinion that it is "divinely inspired." Eusebius mentions that difference of opinion prevailed in his day as to the inspiration of the book, some opposing its claims, and others maintaining its divine origin, especially because it formed an admirable introduction to the Christian faith. For this latter reason it was read publicly, he tells us, in the churches.

The only voice of antiquity decidedly opposed to the claim is that of Tertullian. He designates it apocryphal, and rejects it with scorn, as favouring anti-Montanistic opinions. Even his words, however, show that it was regarded in many churches as Scripture.

The second opinion as to the authorship is found in no writer of any name. It occurs only in two places: a poem falsely ascribed to Tertullian, and a fragment published by Muratori, on the Canon, the authorship of which is unknown, and the original language of which is still a matter of dispute. The fragment says, "The Pastor was written very lately in our times, in the city of Rome, by Hermas, while Bishop Pius, his brother, sat in the chair of the Church of the city of Rome."

A third opinion has had advocates in modern times. The Pastor of Hermas is regarded as a fiction, and the person Hermas, who is the principal character, is, according to this opinion, merely the invention of the fiction-writer.

Whatever opinion critics may have in regard to the authorship, there can be but one opinion as to the date. The Pastor of Hermas must have been written at an early period. The fact that it was recognised by Irenæus as Scripture shows that it must have been in circulation long before his time. The most probable date assigned to its composition is the reign of Hadrian, or of Antoninus Pius.

The work is very important in many respects; but especially as reflecting the tone and style of books which interested and instructed the Christians of the second and third centuries.

The Pastor of Hermas was written in Greek. It was well known in the Eastern Churches: it seems to have been but little read in the Western. Yet the work bears traces of having been written in Italy.

For a long time the Pastor of Hermas was known to scholars only in a Latin version, occurring in several mss. with but slight vacations. But within recent times the difficulty of settling the text has been increased by the discovery of various MSS. A Latin translation has been edited, widely differing from the common version. Then a Greek MSS. was said to have been found in Mount Athos, of which Simonides affirmed that he brought away a portion of the original and a copy of the rest. Then a MS. of the Pastor of Hermas was found at the end of the Sinaitic Codex of Tischendorf. And in addition to all these, there is an Æthiopic translation. The discussion of the value of these discoveries is one of the most difficult that can fall to the lot of critics; for it involves not merely an examination of peculiar forms of words and similar criteria, but an investigation into statements made by Simonides and Tischendorf respecting events in their own lives. But whatever may be the conclusions at which the critic arrives, the general reader does not gain or lose much. In all the Greek and Latin forms the Pastor of Hermas is substantially the same. There are many minute differences; but there are scarcely any of importance,—perhaps we should say none.

In this translation the text of Hilgenfeld, which is based on the Sinaitic Codex, has been followed.

The letters Vat. mean the Vatican manuscript, the one from which the common or Vulgate version was usually printed.

The letters Pal. mean the Palatine manuscript edited by Dressel, which contains the Latin version, differing considerably from the common version.

The letters Lips. refer to the Leipzig manuscript, partly original and partly copied, furnished by Simonides from Athos. The text of Anger and Dindorf (Lips., 1856) has been used, though reference has also been made to the text of Tischendorf in Dressel.

The letters Sin. refer to the Sinaitic Codex, as given in Dressel and in Hilgenfeld's notes.

The letters Æth. refer to the Æthiopic version, edited, with a Latin translation, by Antonius D'Abbadie. Leipzig, 1860.

No attempt has been made to give even a tithe of the various readings. Only the most important have been noted.

[It is but just to direct the reader's attention to an elaborate article of Dr. Donaldson, in the (London) Theological Review, vol. xiv. p. 564; in which he very ingeniously supports his opinions with regard to Hermas, and also touching the Muratorian Canon. In one important particular he favours my own impression; viz., that The Shepherd is a compilation, traditional, or reproduced from memory. He supposes its sentiments "must have been expressed in innumerable oral communications delivered in the churches throughout the world."]

Book of Visions

Vision First

Against Filthy and Proud Thoughts, and the Carelessness of Hermas in Chastising His Sons

CHAPTER I

He who had brought me up, sold me to one Rhode in Rome. Many years after this I recognised her, and I began to love her as a sister. Some time after, I saw her bathe in the river Tiber; and I gave her my hand, and drew her out of the river. The sight of her beauty made me think with myself, "I should be a happy man if I could but get a wife as handsome and good as she is." This was the only thought that passed through me: this and nothing more. A short time after this, as I was walking on my road to the villages, and magnifying the creatures of God, and thinking how magnificent, and beautiful, and powerful they are, I fell asleep. And the Spirit carried me away, and took me through a pathless place, through which a man could not travel, for it was situated in the midst of rocks; it was rugged and impassible on account of water. Having passed over this river, I came to a plain. I then bent down on my knees, and began to pray to the Lord, and to confess my sins. And as I prayed, the heavens were opened, and I see the woman whom I had desired saluting me from the sky, and saying, "Hail, Hermas!" And looking up to her, I said, "Lady, what doest thou here?" And she answered me, "I have been taken up here to accuse you of your sins before the Lord." "Lady," said I, "are you to be the subject of my accusation?" "No," said she; "but hear the words which I am going to speak to you. God, who dwells in the heavens, and made out of nothing the things that exist, and multiplied and increased them on account of His holy Church, is angry with you for having sinned against me." I answered her, "Lady, have I sinned against you? How? or when spoke I an unseemly word to you? Did I not always think of you as a lady? Did I not always respect you as a sister? Why do you falsely accuse me of this wickedness and impurity?" With a smile she replied to me, "The desire of wickedness arose within your heart. Is it not your opinion that a righteous man commits sin when an evil desire arises in his heart? There is sin in such a case, and the sin is great," said she; "for the thoughts of a righteous man should be righteous. For by thinking righteously his character is established in the heavens, and he has the Lord merciful to him in every business. But such as entertain wicked thoughts in their minds are bringing upon themselves death and captivity; and especially is this the case with those who set their affections on this world, and glory in their riches, and look not forward to the blessings of the life to come. For many will their regrets be; for they have no hope, but have despaired of themselves and their life. But do thou pray to God, and He will heal thy sins, and the sins of thy whole house, and of all the saints."

CHAPTER II

After she had spoken these words, the heavens were shut. I was overwhelmed with sorrow and fear, and said to myself, "If this sin is assigned to me, how can I be saved, or how shall I propitiate God in regard to my sins, which are of the grossest character? With what words shall I ask the Lord to be merciful to me?" While I was thinking over these things, and discussing them in my mind, I saw opposite to me a chair, white, made of white wool, of great size. And there came up an old woman, arrayed in a splendid robe, and with a book in her hand; and she sat down alone, and saluted me, "Hail, Hermas!" And in sadness and tears I said to her, "Lady, hail!" And she said to me, "Why are you downcast, Hermas? for you were wont to be patient and temperate, and always smiling. Why are you so gloomy, and not cheerful?" I answered her and said, "O Lady, I have been reproached by a very good woman, who says that I sinned against her." And she said, "Far be such a deed from a servant of God. But perhaps a desire after her has arisen within your heart. Such a wish, in the case of the servants of God, produces sin. For it is a wicked and horrible wish in an all-chaste and already well-tried spirit to desire an evil deed; and especially for Hermas so to do, who keeps himself from all wicked desire, and is full of all simplicity, and of great guilelessness."

CHAPTER III

"But God is not angry with you on account of this, but that you may convert your house, which have committed iniquity against the Lord, and against you, their parents. And although you love your sons, yet did you not warn your house, but permitted them to be terribly corrupted. On this account is the Lord angry with you, but He will heal all the evils which have been done in your house. For, on account of their sins and iniquities, you have been destroyed by the affairs of this world. But now the mercy of the Lord has taken pity on you and your house, and will strengthen you, and establish you in his glory. Only be not easy-minded, but be of good courage and comfort your house. For as a smith hammers out his work, and accomplishes whatever he wishes, so shall righteous daily speech overcome all iniquity. Cease not therefore to admonish your sons; for I know that, if they will repent with all their heart, they will be enrolled in the Books of Life with the saints." Having ended these words, she said to me, "Do you wish to hear me read?" I say to her, "Lady, I do." "Listen then, and give ear to the glories of God." And then I heard from her, magnificently and admirably, things which my memory could not retain. For all the words were terrible, such as man could not endure. The last words, however, I did remember; for they were useful to us, and gentle. "Lo, the God of powers, who by His invisible strong power and great wisdom has created the world, and by His glorious counsel has surrounded His creation with beauty, and by His strong word has fixed the heavens and laid the foundations of the earth upon the waters, and by His own wisdom and providence has created His holy Church, which He has blessed, lo! He removes the heavens and the mountains, the hills and the seas, and all things become plain to His elect, that He may bestow on them the blessing which He has promised them, with much glory and joy, if only they shall keep the commandments of God which they have received in great faith."

CHAPTER IV

When she had ended her reading, she rose from the chair, and four young men came and carried off the chair and went away to the east. And she called me to herself and touched my breast, and said to me, "Have you been pleased with my reading?" And I say to her, "Lady, the last words please me, but the first are cruel and harsh." Then she said to me, "The last are for the righteous: the first are for heathens and apostates." And while she spoke to me, two men appeared and raised her on their shoulders, and they went to where the chair was in the east. With joyful countenance did she depart; and as she went, she said to me, "Behave like a man, Hermas."

Vision Second

Again, of His Neglect in Chastising His Talkative Wife and His Lustful Sons, and of His Character

CHAPTER I

As I was going to the country about the same time as on the previous year, in my walk I recalled to memory the vision of that year. And again the Spirit carried me away, and took me to the same place where I had been the year before. On coming to that place, I bowed my knees and began to pray to the Lord, and to glorify His name, because He had deemed me worthy, and had made known to me my former sins. On rising from prayer, I see opposite me that old woman, whom I had seen the year before, walking and reading some book. And she says to me, "Can you carry a report of these things to the elect of God?" I say to her, "Lady, so much I cannot retain in my memory, but give me the book and I shall transcribe it." "Take it," says she, "and you will give it back to me." Thereupon I took it, and going away into a certain part of the country, I transcribed the whole of it letter by letter; but the syllables of it I did not catch. No sooner, however, had I finished the writing of the book, than all of a sudden it was snatched from my hands; but who the person was that snatched it, I saw not.

CHAPTER II

Fifteen days after, when I had fasted and prayed much to the Lord, the knowledge of the writing was revealed to me. Now the writing was to this effect: "Your seed, O Hermas, has sinned against God, and they have blasphemed against the Lord, and in their great wickedness they have betrayed their parents. And they passed as traitors of their parents, and by their treachery did they not reap profit. And even now they have added to their sins lusts and iniquitous pollutions, and thus their iniquities have been filled up. But make known these words to all your children, and to your wife, who is to be your sister. For she does not restrain her tongue, with which she commits iniquity; but, on hearing these words, she will control herself, and will obtain mercy. For after you have made known to them these words which my Lord has commanded me to reveal to you, then shall they be forgiven all the sins which in former times they committed, and forgiveness will be granted to all the saints who have sinned even to the present day, if they repent with all their heart, and drive all doubts from their minds. For the Lord has sworn by His glory, in regard to His elect, that if any one of them sin after a certain day which has been fixed, he shall not be saved. For the repentance of the righteous has limits. Filled up are the days of repentance to all the saints; but to the heathen, repentance will be possible even to the last day. You will tell, therefore, those who preside over the Church, to direct their ways in righteousness, that they may receive in full the promises with great glory. Stand stedfast, therefore, ye who work righteousness, and doubt not, that your passage may be with the holy angels. Happy ye who endure the great tribulation that is coming on, and happy they who shall not deny their own life. For the Lord hath sworn by His Son, that those who denied their Lord have abandoned their life in despair, for even now these are to deny Him in the days that are coming. To those who denied in earlier times, God became gracious, on account of His exceeding tender mercy."

CHAPTER III

"But as for you, Hermas, remember not the wrongs done to you by your children, nor neglect your sister, that they may be cleansed from their former sins. For they will be instructed with righteous instruction, if you remember not the wrongs they have done you. For the remembrance of wrongs worketh death. And you, Hermas, have endured great personal tribulations on account of the transgressions of your house, because you did not attend to them, but were careless and engaged in your wicked transactions. But you are saved, because you did not depart from the living God, and on account of your simplicity and great self-control. These have saved you, if you remain stedfast. And they will save all who act in the same manner, and walk in guilelessness and simplicity. Those who possess such virtues will wax strong against every form of wickedness, and will abide unto eternal life. Blessed are all they who practice righteousness, for they shall never be destroyed. Now you will tell Maximus: Lo! tribulation cometh on. If it seemeth good to thee, deny again. The Lord is near to them who return unto Him, as it is written in Eldad and Modat, who prophesied to the people in the wilderness."

CHAPTER IV

Now a revelation was given to me, my brethren, while I slept, by a young man of comely appearance, who said to me, "Who do you think that old woman is from whom you received the book?" And I said, "The Sibyl." "You are in a mistake," says he; "it is not the Sibyl." "Who is it then?" say I. And he said, "It is the Church." And I said to him, "Why then is she an old woman?" "Because," said he, "she was created first of all. On this account is she old. And for her sake was the world made." After that I saw a vision in my house, and that old woman came and asked me, if I had yet given the book to the presbyters. And I said that I had not. And then she said, "You have done well, for I have some words to add. But when I finish all the words, all the elect will then become acquainted with them through you. You will write therefore two books, and you will send the one to Clemens and the other to Grapte. And Clemens will send his to foreign countries, for permission has been granted to him to do so. And Grapte will admonish the widows and the orphans. But you will read the words in this city, along with the presbyters who preside over the Church."

Vision Third

Concerning the Building of the Triumphant Church, and the Various Classes of Reprobate Men

CHAPTER I

The vision which I saw, my brethren, was of the following nature. Having fasted frequently, and having prayed to the Lord that He would show me the revelation which He promised to show me through that old woman, the same night that old woman appeared to me, and said to me, "Since you are so anxious and eager to know all things, go into the part of the country where you tarry; and about the fifth hour I shall appear unto you, and show you all that you ought to see." I asked her, saying "Lady, into what part of the country am I to go?" And she said, "Into any part you wish." Then I chose a spot which was suitable, and retired. Before, however, I began to speak and to mention the place, she said to me, "I will come where you wish." Accordingly, I went to the country, and counted the hours, and reached the place where I had promised to meet her. And I see an ivory seat ready placed, and on it a linen cushion, and above the linen cushion was spread a covering of fine linen. Seeing these laid out, and yet no one in the place, I began to feel awe, and as it were a trembling seized hold of me, and my hair stood on end, and as it were a horror came upon me when I saw that I was all alone. But on coming back to myself and calling to mind the glory of God, I took courage, bent my knees, and again confessed my sins to God as I had done before. Whereupon the old woman approached, accompanied by six young men whom I had also seen before; and she stood behind me, and listened to me, as I prayed and confessed my sins to the Lord. And touching me she said, "Hermas, cease praying continually for your sins; pray for righteousness, that you may have a portion of it immediately in your house." On this, she took me up by the hand, and brought me to the seat, and said to the young men, "Go and build." When the young men had gone and we were alone, she said to me, "Sit here." I say to her, "Lady, permit my elders to be seated first." "Do what I bid you," said she; "sit down." When I would have sat down on her right, she did not permit me, but with her hand beckoned to me to sit down on the left. While I was thinking about this, and feeling vexed that she did not let me sit on the right, she said, "Are you vexed, Hermas? The place to the right is for others who have already pleased God, and have suffered for His name's sake; and you have yet much to accomplish before you can sit with them. But abide as you now do in your simplicity, and you will sit with them, and with all who do their deeds and bear what they have borne."

CHAPTER II

"What have they borne?" said I. "Listen," said she: "scourges, prisons, great tribulations, crosses, wild beasts, for God's name's sake. On this account is assigned to them the division of sanctification on the right hand, and to every one who shall suffer for God's name: to the rest is assigned the division on the left. But both for those who sit on the right, and those who sit on the left, there are the same gifts and promises; only those sit on the right, and have some glory. You then are eager to sit on the right with them, but your shortcomings are many. But you will be cleansed from your shortcomings; and all who are not given to doubts shall be cleansed from all their iniquities up till this day." Saying this, she wished to go away. But falling down at her feet, I begged her by the Lord that she would show me the vision which she had promised to show me. And then she again took hold of me by the hand, and raised me, and made me sit on the seat to the left; and lifting up a splendid rod, she said to me, "Do you see something great?" And I say, "Lady, I see nothing." She said to me, "Lo! do you not see opposite to you a great tower, built upon the waters, of splendid square stones?" For the tower was built square by those six young men who had come with her. But myriads of men were carrying stones to it, some dragging them from the depths, others removing them from the land, and they handed them to these six young men. They were taking them and building; and those of the stones that were dragged out of the depths, they placed in the building just as they were: for they were polished and fitted exactly into the other stones, and became so united one with another that the lines of juncture could not be perceived. And in this way the building of the tower looked as if it were made out of one stone. Those stones, however, which were taken from the earth suffered a different fate; for the young men rejected some of them, some they fitted into the building, and some they cut down, and cast far away from the tower. Many other stones, however, lay around the tower, and the young men did not use them in building; for some of them were rough, others had cracks in them, others had been made too short, and others were white and round, but did not fit into the building of the tower. Moreover, I saw other stones thrown far away from the tower, and falling into the public road; yet they did not remain on the road, but were rolled into a pathless place. And I saw others falling into the fire and burning, others falling close to the water, and yet not capable of being rolled into the water, though they wished to be rolled down, and to enter the water.

CHAPTER III

On showing me these visions, she wished to retire. I said to her, "What is the use of my having seen all this, while I do not know what it means?" She said to me, "You are a cunning fellow, wishing to know everything that relates to the tower." "Even so, O Lady," said I, "that I may tell it to my brethren, that, hearing this, they may know the Lord in much glory." And she said, "Many indeed shall hear, and hearing, some shall be glad, and some shall weep. But even these, if they hear and repent, shall also rejoice. Hear, then, the parables of the tower; for I will reveal all to you, and give me no more trouble in regard to revelation: for these revelations have an end, for they have been completed. But you will not cease praying for revelations, for you are shameless. The tower which you see building is myself, the Church, who have appeared to you now and on the former occasion. Ask, then, whatever you like in regard to the tower, and I will reveal it to you, that you may rejoice with the saints." I said unto her, "Lady, since you have vouchsafed to reveal all to me this once, reveal it." She said to me, "Whatsoever ought to be revealed, will be revealed; only let your heart be with God, and doubt not whatsoever you shall see." I asked her, "Why was the tower built upon the waters, O Lady?" She answered, "I told you before, and you still inquire carefully: therefore inquiring you shall find the truth. Hear then why the tower is built upon the waters. It is because your life has been, and will be, saved through water. For the tower was founder on the word of the almighty and glorious Name and it is kept together by the invisible power of the Lord."

CHAPTER IV

In reply I said to her, "This is magnificent and marvellous. But who are the six young men who are engaged in building?" And she said, "These are the holy angels of God, who were first created, and to whom the Lord handed over His whole creation, that they might increase and build up and rule over the whole creation. By these will the building of the tower be finished." "But who are the other persons who are engaged in carrying the stones?" "These also are holy angels of the Lord, but the former six are more excellent than these. The building of the tower will be finished, and all will rejoice together around the tower, and they will glorify God, because the tower is finished." I asked her, saying, "Lady, I should like to know what became of the stones, and what was meant by the various kinds of stones?" In reply she said to me, "Not because you are more deserving than all others that this revelation should be made to you—for there are others before you, and better than you, to whom these visions should have been revealed—but that the name of God may be glorified, has the revelation been made to you, and it will be made on account of the doubtful who ponder in their hearts whether these things will be or not. Tell them that all these things are true, and that none of them is beyond the truth. All of them are firm and sure, and established on a strong foundation."

CHAPTER V

"Hear now with regard to the stones which are in the building. Those square white stones which fitted exactly into each other, are apostles, bishops, teachers, and deacons, who have lived in godly purity, and have acted as bishops and teachers and deacons chastely and reverently to the elect of God. Some of them have fallen asleep, and some still remain alive. And they have always agreed with each other, and been at peace among themselves, and listened to each other. On account of this, they join exactly into the building of the tower." "But who are the stones that were dragged from the depths, and which were laid into the building and fitted in with the rest of the stones previously placed in the tower?" "They are those who suffered for the Lord's sake." "But I wish to know, O Lady, who are the other stones which were carried from the land." "Those," she said, "which go into the building without being polished, are those whom God has approved of, for they walked in the straight ways of the Lord and practiced His commandments." "But who are those who are in the act of being brought and placed in the building?" "They are those who are young in faith and are faithful. But they are admonished by the angels to do good, for no iniquity has been found in them." "Who then are those whom they rejected and cast away?" "These are they who have sinned, and wish to repent. On this account they have not been thrown far from the tower, because they will yet be useful in the building, if they repent. Those then who are to repent, if they do repent, will be strong in faith, if they now repent while the tower is building. For if the building be finished, there will not be more room for any one, but he will be rejected. This privilege, however, will belong only to him who has now been placed near the tower."

CHAPTER VI

"As to those who were cut down and thrown far away from the tower, do you wish to know who they are? They are the sons of iniquity, and they believed in hypocrisy, and wickedness did not depart from them. For this reason they are not saved, since they cannot be used in the building on account of their iniquities. Wherefore they have been cut off and cast far away on account of the anger of the Lord, for they have roused Him to anger. But I shall explain to you the other stones which you saw lying in great numbers, and not going into the building. Those which are rough are those who have known the truth and not remained in it, nor have they been joined to the saints. On this account are they unfit for use." "Who are those that have rents?" "These are they who are at discord in their hearts one with another, and are not at peace amongst themselves: they indeed keep peace before each other, but when they separate one from the other, their wicked thoughts remain in their hearts. These, then, are the rents which are in the stones. But those which are shortened are those who have indeed believed, and have the larger share of righteousness; yet they have also a considerable share of iniquity, and therefore they are shortened and not whole." "But who are these, Lady, that are white and round, and yet do not fit into the building of the tower?" She answered and said, "How long will you be foolish and stupid, and continue to put every kind of question and understand nothing? These are those who have faith indeed, but they have also the riches of this world. When, therefore, tribulation comes, on account of their riches and business they deny the Lord." I answered and said to her, "When, then, will they be useful for the building, Lady?" "When the riches that now seduce them have been circumscribed, then will they be of use to God. For as a round stone cannot become square unless portions be cut off and cast away, so also those who are rich in this world cannot be useful to the Lord unless their riches be cut down. Learn this first from your own case. When you were rich, you were useless; but now you are useful and fit for life. Be ye useful to God; for you also will be used as one of these stones."

CHAPTER VII

"Now the other stones which you saw cast far away from the tower, and falling upon the public road and rolling from it into pathless places, are those who have indeed believed, but through doubt have abandoned the true road. Thinking, then, that they could find a better, they wander and become wretched, and enter upon pathless places. But those which fell into the fire and were burned are those who have departed for ever from the living God; nor does the thought of repentance ever come into their hearts, on account of their devotion to their lusts and to the crimes which they committed. Do you wish to know who are the others which fell near the waters, but could not be rolled into them? These are they who have heard the word, and wish to be baptized in the name of the Lord; but when the chastity demanded by the truth comes into their recollection, they draw back, and again walk after their own wicked desires." She finished her exposition of the tower. But I, shameless as I yet was, asked her, "Is repentance possible for all those stones which have been cast away and did not fit into the building of the tower, and will they yet have a place in this tower?" "Repentance," said she, "is yet possible, but in this tower they cannot find a suitable place. But in another and much inferior place they will be laid, and that, too, only when they have been tortured and completed the days of their sins. And on this account will they be transferred, because they have partaken of the righteous Word. And then only will they be removed from their punishments when the thought of repenting of the evil deeds which they have done has come into their hearts. But if it does not come into their hearts, they will not be saved, on account of the hardness of their heart."

CHAPTER VIII

When then I ceased asking in regard to all these matters, she said to me, "Do you wish to see anything else?" And as I was extremely eager to see something more, my countenance beamed with joy. She looked towards me with a smile, and said, "Do you see seven women around the tower?" "I do, Lady," said I. "This tower," said she, "is supported by them according to the precept of the Lord. Listen now to their functions. The first of them, who is clasping her hands, is called Faith. Through her the elect of God are saved. Another, who has her garments tucked up and acts with vigour, is called Self-restraint. She is the daughter of Faith. Whoever then follows her will become happy in his life, because he will restrain himself from all evil works, believing that, if he restrain himself from all evil desire, he will inherit eternal life." "But the others," said I, "O Lady, who are they?" And she said to me, "They are daughters of each other. One of them is called Simplicity, another Guilelessness, another Chastity, another Intelligence, another Love. When then you do all the works of their mother, you will be able to live." "I should like to know," said I, "O Lady, what power each one of them possesses." "Hear," she said, "what power they have. Their powers are regulated by each other, and follow each other in the order of their birth. For from Faith arises Self-restraint; from Self-restraint, Simplicity; from Simplicity, Guilelessness; from Guilelessness, Chastity; from Chastity, Intelligence; and from Intelligence, Love. The deeds, then, of these are pure, and chaste, and divine. Whoever devotes himself to these, and is able to hold fast by their works, shall have his dwelling in the tower with the saints of God." Then I asked her in regard to the ages, if now there is the conclusion. She cried out with a loud voice, "Foolish man! do you not see the tower yet building? When the tower is finished and built, then comes the end; and I assure you it will be soon finished. Ask me no more questions. Let you and all the saints be content with what I have called to your remembrance, and with my renewal of your spirits. But observe that it is not for your own sake only that these revelations have been made to you, but they have been given you that you may show them to all. For after three days—this you will take care to remember—I Command you to speak all the words which I am to say to you into the ears of the saints, that hearing them and doing them, they may be cleansed from their iniquities, and you along with them."

CHAPTER IX

Give ear unto me, O Sons: I have brought you up in much simplicity, and guilelessness, and chastity, on account of the mercy of the Lord, who has dropped His righteousness down upon you, that ye may be made righteous and holy from all your iniquity and depravity; but you do not wish to rest from your iniquity. Now, therefore, listen to me, and be at peace one with another, and visit each other, and bear each other's burdens, and do not partake of God's creatures alone, but give abundantly of them to the needy. For some through the abundance of their food produce weakness in their flesh, and thus corrupt their flesh; while the flesh of others who have no food is corrupted, because they have not sufficient nourishment. And on this account their bodies waste away. This intemperance in eating is thus injurious to you who have abundance and do not distribute among those who are needy. Give heed to the judgment that is to come. Ye, therefore, who are high in position, seek out the hungry as long as the tower is not yet finished; for after the tower is finished, you will wish to do good, but will find no opportunity. Give heed, therefore, ye who glory in your wealth, lest those who are needy should groan, and their groans should ascend to the Lord, and ye be shut out with all your goods beyond the gate of the tower. Wherefore I now say to you who preside over the Church and love the first seats, "Be not like to drug-mixers. For the drug-mixers carry their drugs in boxes, but ye carry your drug and poison in your heart. Ye are hardened, and do not wish to cleanse your hearts, and to add unity of aim to purity of heart, that you may have mercy from the great King. Take heed, therefore, children, that these dissensions of yours do not deprive you of your life. How will you instruct the elect of the Lord, if you yourselves have not instruction? Instruct each other therefore, and be at peace among yourselves, that I also, standing joyful before your Father, may give an account of you all to your Lord."

CHAPTER X

On her ceasing to speak to me, those six young men who were engaged in building came and conveyed her to the tower, and other four lifted up the seat and carried it also to the tower. The faces of these last I did not see, for they were turned away from me. And as she was going, I asked her to reveal to me the meaning of the three forms in which she appeared to me. In reply she said to me: "With regard to them, you must ask another to reveal their meaning to you." For she had appeared to me, brethren, in the first vision the previous year under the form of an exceedingly old woman, sitting in a chair. In the second vision her face was youthful, but her skin and hair betokened age, and she stood while she spoke to me. She was also more joyful than on the first occasion. But in the third vision she was entirely youthful and exquisitely beautiful, except only that she had the hair of an old woman; but her face beamed with joy, and she sat on a seat. Now I was exceeding sad in regard to these appearances, for I longed much to know what the visions meant. Then I see the old woman in a vision of the night saying unto me: "Every prayer should be accompanied with humility: fast, therefore, and you will obtain from the Lord what you beg." I fasted therefore for one day.

That very night there appeared to me a young man, who said, "Why do you frequently ask revelations in prayer? Take heed lest by asking many things you injure your flesh: be content with these revelations. Will you be able to see greater revelations than those which you have seen?" I answered and said to him, "Sir, one thing only I ask, that in regard to these three forms the revelation may be rendered complete." He answered me, "How long are ye senseless? But your doubts make you senseless, because you have not your hearts turned towards the Lord." But I answered and said to him, "From you, sir, we shall learn these things more accurately."

CHAPTER XI

"Hear then," said he, "with regard to the three forms, concerning which you are inquiring. Why in the first vision did she appear to you as an old woman seated on a chair? Because your spirit is now old and withered up, and has lost its power in consequence of your infirmities and doubts. For, like elderly men who have no hope of renewing their strength, and expect nothing but their last sleep, so you, weakened by worldly occupations, have given yourselves up to sloth, and have not cast your cares upon the Lord. Your spirit therefore is broken, and you have grown old in your sorrows." "I should like then to know, sir, why she sat on a chair?" He answered, "Because every weak person sits on a chair on account of his weakness, that his weakness may be sustained. Lo! you have the form of the first vision."

CHAPTER XII

"Now in the second vision you saw her standing with a youthful countenance, and more joyful than before; still she had the skin and hair of an aged woman. Hear," said he, "this parable also. When one becomes somewhat old, he despairs of himself on account of his weakness and poverty, and looks forward to nothing but the last day of his life. Then suddenly an inheritance is left him: and hearing of this, he rises up, and becoming exceeding joyful, he puts on strength. And now he no longer reclines, but stands up; and his spirit, already destroyed by his previous actions, is renewed, and he no longer sits, but acts with vigour. So happened it with you on hearing the revelation which God gave you. For the Lord had compassion on you, and renewed your spirit, and ye laid aside your infirmities. Vigour arose within you, and ye grew strong in faith; and the Lord, seeing your strength, rejoiced. On this account He showed you the building of the tower; and He will show you other things, if you continue at peace with each other with all your heart."

CHAPTER XIII

"Now, in the third vision, you saw her still younger, and she was noble and joyful, and her shape was beautiful. For, just as when some good news comes suddenly to one who is sad, immediately he forgets his former sorrows, and looks for nothing else than the good news which he has heard, and for the future is made strong for good, and his spirit is renewed on account of the joy which he has received; so ye also have received the renewal of your spirits by seeing these good things. As to your seeing her sitting on a seat, that means that her position is one of strength, for a seat has four feet and stands firmly. For the world also is kept together by means of four elements. Those, therefore, who repent completely and with the whole heart, will become young and firmly established. You now have the revelation completely given you. Make no further demands for revelations. If anything ought to be revealed, it will be revealed to you."

Vision Fourth

Concerning the Trial and Tribulation that are to Come Upon Men

CHAPTER I

Twenty days after the former vision I saw another vision, brethren—a representation of the tribulation that is to come. I was going to a country house along the Campanian road. Now the house lay about ten furlongs from the public road. The district is one rarely traversed. And as I walked alone, I prayed the Lord to complete the revelations which He had made to me through His holy Church, that He might strengthen me, and give repentance to all His servants who were going astray, that His great and glorious name might be glorified because He vouchsafed to show me His marvels. And while I was glorifying Him and giving Him thanks, a voice, as it were, answered me, "Doubt not, Hermas;" and I began to think with myself, and to say, "What reason have I to doubt—I who have been established by the Lord, and who have seen such glorious sights?" I advanced a little, brethren, and, lo! I see dust rising even to the heavens. I began to say to myself, "Are cattle approaching and raising the dust?" It was about a furlong's distance from me. And, lo! I see the dust rising more and more, so that I imagined that it was something sent from God. But the sun now shone out a little, and, lo! I see a mighty beast like a whale, and out of its mouth fiery locusts proceeded. But the size of that beast was about a hundred feet, and it had a head like an urn. I began to weep, and to call on the Lord to rescue me from it. Then I remembered the word which I had heard, "Doubt not, O Hermas." Clothed, therefore, my brethren, with faith in the Lord and remembering the great things which He had taught me, I boldly faced the beast. Now that beast came on with such noise and force, that it could itself have destroyed a city. I came near it, and the monstrous beast stretched itself out on the ground, and showed nothing but its tongue, and did not stir at all until I had passed by it. Now the beast had four colours on its head—black, then fiery and bloody, then golden, and lastly white.

CHAPTER II

Now after I had passed by the wild beast, and had moved forward about thirty feet, lo! a virgin meets me, adorned as if she were proceeding from the bridal chamber, clothed entirely in white, and with white sandals, and veiled up to her forehead, and her head was covered by a hood. And she had white hair. I knew from my former visions that this was the Church, and I became more joyful. She saluted me, and said, "Hail, O man!" And I returned her salutation, and said, "Lady, hail!" And she answered, and said to me, "Has nothing crossed your path?" I say, "I was met by a beast of such a size that it could destroy peoples, but through the power of the Lord and His great mercy I escaped from it." "Well did you escape from it," says she, "because you cast your care on God, and opened your heart to the Lord, believing that you can be saved by no other than by His great and glorious name. On this account the Lord has sent His angel, who has rule over the beasts, and whose name is Thegri, and has shut up its mouth, so that it cannot tear you. You have escaped from great tribulation on account of your faith, and because you did not doubt in the presence of such a beast. Go, therefore, and tell the elect of the Lord His mighty deeds, and say to them that this beast is a type of the great tribulation that is coming. If then ye prepare yourselves, and repent with all your heart, and turn to the Lord, it will be possible for you to escape it, if your heart be pure and spotless, and ye spend the rest of the days of your life in serving the Lord blamelessly. Cast your cares upon the Lord, and He will direct them. Trust the Lord, ye who doubt, for He is all-powerful, and can turn His anger away from you, and send scourges on the doubters. Woe to those who hear these words, and despise them: better were it for them not to have been born."

CHAPTER III

I asked her about the four colours which the beast had on his head. And she answered, and said to me, "Again you are inquisitive in regard to such matters." "Yea, Lady," said I, "make known to me what they are." "Listen," said she: "the black is the world in which we dwell: but the fiery and bloody points out that the world must perish through blood and fire: but the golden part are you who have escaped from this world. For as gold is tested by fire, and thus becomes useful, so are you tested who dwell in it. Those, therefore, who continue stedfast, and are put through the fire, will be purified by means of it. For as gold casts away its dross, so also will ye cast away all sadness and straitness, and will be made pure so as to fit into the building of the tower. But the white part is the age that is to come, in which the elect of God will dwell, since those elected by God to eternal life will be spotless and pure. Wherefore cease not speaking these things into the ears of the saints. This then is the type of the great tribulation that is to come. If ye wish it, it will be nothing. Remember those things which were written down before." And saying this, she departed. But I saw not into what place she retired. There was a noise, however, and I turned round in alarm, thinking that that beast was coming.

Vision Fifth

Concerning the Commandments.

After I had been praying at home, and had sat down on my couch, there entered a man of glorious aspect, dressed like a shepherd, with a white goat's skin, a wallet on his shoulders, and a rod in his hand, and saluted me. I returned his salutation. And straightway he sat down beside me, and said to me, "I have been sent by a most venerable angel to dwell with you the remaining days of your life." And I thought that he had come to tempt me, and I said to him, "Who are you? For I know him to whom I have been entrusted." He said to me, "Do you not know me?" "No," said I. "I," said he, "am that shepherd to whom you have been entrusted." And while he yet spake, his figure was changed; and then I knew that it was he to whom I had been entrusted. And straightway I became confused, and fear took hold of me, and I was overpowered with deep sorrow that I had answered him so wickedly and foolishly. But he answered, and said to me, "Do not be confounded, but receive strength from the commandments which I am going to give you. For I have been sent," said he, "to show you again all the things which you saw before, especially those of them which are useful to you. First of all, then, write down my commandments and similitudes, and you will write the other things as I shall show you. For this purpose," said he, "I command you to write down the commandments and similitudes first, that you may read them easily, and be able to keep them." Accordingly I wrote down the commandments and similitudes, exactly as he had ordered me. If then, when you have heard these, ye keep them and walk in them, and practice them with pure minds, you will receive from the Lord all that He has promised to you. But if, after you have heard them, ye do not repent, but continue to add to your sins, then shall ye receive from the Lord the opposite things. All these words did the shepherd, even the angel of repentance, command me to write.

Book of Mandates

Commandment First

On Faith in God

First of all, believe that there is one God who created and finished all things, and made all things out of nothing. He alone is able to contain the whole, but Himself cannot be contained. Have faith therefore in Him, and fear Him; and fearing Him, exercise self-control. Keep these commands, and you will cast away from you all wickedness, and put on the strength of righteousness, and live to God, if you keep this commandment.

Commandment Second

On Avoiding Evil-Speaking, and on Giving Alms in Simplicity

He said to me, "Be simple and guileless, and you will be as the children who know not the wickedness that ruins the life of men. First, then, speak evil of no one, nor listen with pleasure to any one who speaks evil of another. But if you listen, you will partake of the sin of him who speaks evil, if you believe the slander which you hear; for believing it, you will also have something to say against your brother. Thus, then, will you be guilty of the sin of him who slanders. For slander is evil and an unsteady demon. It never abides in peace, but always remains in discord. Keep yourself from it, and you will always be at peace with all. Put on a holiness in which there is no wicked cause of offence, but all deeds that are equable and joyful. Practise goodness; and from the rewards of your labours, which God gives you, give to all the needy in simplicity, not hesitating as to whom you are to give or not to give. Give to all, for God wishes His gifts to be shared amongst all. They who receive, will render an account to God why and for what they have received. For the afflicted who receive will not be condemned, but they who receive on false pretences will suffer punishment. He, then, who gives is guiltless. For as he received from the Lord, so has he accomplished his service in simplicity, not hesitating as to whom he should give and to whom he should not give. This service, then, if accomplished in simplicity, is glorious with God. He, therefore, who thus ministers in simplicity, will live to God. Keep therefore these commandments, as I have given them to you, that your repentance and the repentance of your house may be found in simplicity, and your heart may be pure and stainless."

Commandment Third

On Avoiding Falsehood, and on the Repentance of Hermas for His Dissimulation

Again he said to me, "Love the truth, and let nothing but truth proceed from your mouth, that the spirit which God has placed in your flesh may be found truthful before all men; and the Lord, who dwelleth in you, will be glorified, because the Lord is truthful in every word, and in Him is no falsehood. They therefore who lie deny the Lord, and rob Him, not giving back to Him the deposit which they have received. For they received from Him a spirit free from falsehood. If they give him back this spirit untruthful, they pollute the commandment of the Lord, and become robbers." On hearing these words, I wept most violently. When he saw me weeping, he said to me, "Why do you weep?" And I said, "Because, sir, I know not if I can be saved." "Why?" said he. And I said, "Because, sir, I never spake a true word in my life, but have ever spoken cunningly to all, and have affirmed a lie for the truth to all; and no one ever contradicted me, but credit was given to my word. How then can I live, since I have acted thus?" And he said to me, "Your feelings are indeed right and sound, for you ought as a servant of God to have walked in truth, and not to have joined an evil conscience with the spirit of truth, nor to have caused sadness to the holy and true Spirit." And I said to him, "Never, sir, did I listen to these words with so much attention." And he said to me, "Now you hear them, and keep them, that even the falsehoods which you formerly told in your transactions may come to be believed through the truthfulness of your present statements. For even they can become worthy of credit. If you keep these precepts, and from this time forward you speak nothing but the truth, it will be possible for you to obtain life. And whosoever shall hear this commandment, and depart from that great wickedness falsehood, shall live to God."

Commandment Fourth

On Putting One's Wife Away for Adultery

CHAPTER I

"I charge you," said he, "to guard your chastity, and let no thought enter your heart of another man's wife, or of fornication, or of similar iniquities; for by doing this you commit a great sin. But if you always remember your own wife, you will never sin. For if this thought enter your heart, then you will sin; and if, in like manner, you think other wicked thoughts, you commit sin. For this thought is great sin in a servant of God. But if any one commit this wicked deed, he works death for himself. Attend, therefore, and refrain from this thought; for where purity dwells, there iniquity ought not to enter the heart of a righteous man." I said to him, "Sir, permit me to ask you a few questions." "Say on," said he. And I said to him, "Sir, if any one has a wife who trusts in the Lord, and if he detect her in adultery, does the man sin if he continue to live with her?" And he said to me, "As long as he remains ignorant of her sin, the husband commits no transgression in living with her. But if the husband know that his wife has gone astray, and if the woman does not repent, but persists in her fornication, and yet the husband continues to live with her, he also is guilty of her crime, and a sharer in her adultery." And I said to him, "What then, sir, is the husband to do, if his wife continue in her vicious practices?" And he said, "The husband should put her away, and remain by himself. But if he put his wife away and marry another, he also commits adultery." And I said to him, "What if the woman put away should repent, and wish to return to her husband: shall she not be taken back by her husband?" And he said to me, "Assuredly. If the husband do not take her back, he sins, and brings a great sin upon himself; for he ought to take back the sinner who has repented. But not frequently. For there is but one repentance to the servants of God. In case, therefore, that the divorced wife may repent, the husband ought not to marry another, when his wife has been put away. In this matter man and woman are to be treated exactly in the same way. Moreover, adultery is committed not only by those who pollute their flesh, but by those who imitate the heathen in their actions. Wherefore if any one persists in such deeds, and repents not, withdraw from him, and cease to live with him, otherwise you are a sharer in his sin. Therefore has the injunction been laid on you, that you should remain by yourselves, both man and woman, for in such persons repentance can take place. But I do not," said he, "give opportunity for the doing of these deeds, but that he who has sinned may sin no more. But with regard to his previous transgressions, there is One who is able to provide a cure; for it is He, indeed, who has power over all."

CHAPTER II

I asked him again, and said, "Since the Lord has vouchsafed to dwell always with me, bear with me while I utter a few words; for I understand nothing, and my heart has been hardened by my previous mode of life. Give me understanding, for I am exceedingly dull, and I understand absolutely nothing." And he answered and said unto me, "I am set over repentance, and I give understanding to all who repent. Do you not think," he said, "that it is great wisdom to repent? for repentance is great wisdom. For he who has sinned understands that he acted wickedly in the sight of the Lord, and remembers the actions he has done, and he repents, and no longer acts wickedly, but does good munificently, and humbles and torments his soul because he has sinned. You see, therefore, that repentance is great wisdom." And I said to him, "It is for this reason, sir, that I inquire carefully into all things, especially because I am a sinner; that I may know what works I should do, that I may live: for my sins are many and various." And he said to me, "You shall live if you keep my commandments, and walk in them; and whosoever shall hear and keep these commandments, shall live to God."

CHAPTER III

And I said to him, "I should like to continue my questions." "Speak on," said he. And I said, "I heard, sir, some teachers maintain that there is no other repentance than that which takes place, when we descended into the water and received remission of our former sins." He said to me, "That was sound doctrine which you heard; for that is really the case. For he who has received remission of his sins ought not to sin any more, but to live in purity. Since, however, you inquire diligently into all things, I will point this also out to you, not as giving occasion for error to those who are to believe, or have lately believed, in the Lord. For those who have now believed, and those who are to believe, have not repentance for their sins; but they have remission of their previous sins. For to those who have been called before these days, the Lord has set repentance. For the Lord, knowing the heart, and foreknowing all things, knew the weakness of men and the manifold wiles of the devil, that he would inflict some evil on the servants of God, and would act wickedly towards them. The Lord, therefore, being merciful, has had mercy on the work of His hand, and has set repentance for them; and He has entrusted to me power over this repentance. And therefore I say to you, that if any one is tempted by the devil, and sins after that great and holy calling in which the Lord has called His people to everlasting life, he has opportunity to repent but once. But if he should sin frequently after this, and then repent, to such a man his repentance will be of no avail; for with difficulty will he live." And I said, "Sir, I feel that life has come back to me in listening attentively to these commandments; for I know that I shall be saved, if in future I sin no more." And he said, "You will be saved, you and all who keep these commandments."

CHAPTER IV

And again I asked him, saying, "Sir, since you have been so patient in listening to me, will you show me this also?" "Speak," said he. And I said, "If a wife or husband die, and the widower or widow marry, does he or she commit sin?" "There is no sin in marrying again," said he; "but if they remain unmarried, they gain greater honour and glory with the Lord; but if they marry, they do not sin. Guard, therefore, your chastity and purity, and you will live to God. What commandments I now give you, and what I am to give, keep from henceforth, yea, from the very day when you were entrusted to me, and I will dwell in your house. And your former sins will be forgiven, if you keep my commandments. And all shall be forgiven who keep these my commandments, and walk in this chastity."

Commandment Fifth

Of Sadness of Heart, and of Patience

CHAPTER I

"Be patient," said he, "and of good understanding, and you will rule over every wicked work, and you will work all righteousness. For if you be patient, the Holy Spirit that dwells in you will be pure. He will not be darkened by any evil spirit, but, dwelling in a broad region, he will rejoice and be glad; and with the vessel in which he dwells he will serve God in gladness, having great peace within himself. But if any outburst of anger take place, forthwith the Holy Spirit, who is tender, is straitened, not having a pure place, and He seeks to depart. For he is choked by the vile spirit, and cannot attend on the Lord as he wishes, for anger pollutes him. For the Lord dwells in long-suffering, but the devil in anger. The two spirits, then, when dwelling in the same habitation, are at discord with each other, and are troublesome to that man in whom they dwell. For if an exceedingly small piece of wormwood be taken and put into a jar of honey, is not the honey entirely destroyed, and does not the exceedingly small piece of wormwood entirely take away the sweetness of the honey, so that it no longer affords any gratification to its owner, but has become bitter, and lost its use? But if the wormwood be not put into the honey, then the honey remains sweet, and is of use to its owner. You see, then, that patience is sweeter than honey, and useful to God, and the Lord dwells in it. But anger is bitter and useless. Now, if anger be mingled with patience, the patience is polluted, and its prayer is not then useful to God." "I should like, sir," said I, "to know the power of anger, that I may guard myself against it." And he said, "If you do not guard yourself against it, you and your house lose all hope of salvation. Guard yourself, therefore, against it. For I am with you, and all will depart from it who repent with their whole heart. For I will be with them, and I will save them all. For all are justified by the most holy angel."

CHAPTER II

"Hear now," said he, "how wicked is the action of anger, and in what way it overthrows the servants of God by its action, and turns them from righteousness. But it does not turn away those who are full of faith, nor does it act on them, for the power of the Lord is with them. It is the thoughtless and doubting that it turns away. For as soon as it sees such men standing stedfast, it throws itself into their hearts, and for nothing at all the man or woman becomes embittered on account of occurrences in their daily life, as for instance on account of their food, or some superfluous word that has been uttered, or on account of some friend, or some gift or debt, or some such senseless affair. For all these things are foolish and empty and unprofitable to the servants of God. But patience is great, and mighty, and strong, and calm in the midst of great enlargement, joyful, rejoicing, free from care, glorifying God at all times, having no bitterness in her, and abiding continually meek and quiet. Now this patience dwells with those who have complete faith. But anger is foolish, and fickle, and senseless. Now, of folly is begotten bitterness, and of bitterness anger, and of anger frenzy. This frenzy, the product of so many evils, ends in great and incurable sin. For when all these spirits dwell in one vessel in which the Holy Spirit also dwells, the vessel cannot contain them, but overflows. The tender Spirit, then, not being accustomed to dwell with the wicked spirit, nor with hardness, withdraws from such a man, and seeks to dwell with meekness and peacefulness. Then, when he withdraws from the man in whom he dwelt, the man is emptied of the righteous Spirit; and being henceforward filled with evil spirits, he is in a state of anarchy in every action, being dragged hither and thither by the evil spirits, and there is a complete darkness in his mind as to everything good. This, then, is what happens to all the angry. Wherefore do you depart from that most wicked spirit anger, and put on patience, and resist anger and bitterness, and you will be found in company with the purity which is loved by the Lord. Take care, then, that you neglect not by any chance this commandment: for if you obey this commandment, you will be able to keep all the other commandments which I am to give you. Be strong, then, in these commandments, and put on power, and let all put on power, as many as wish to walk in them."

Commandment Sixth

How to Recognise the Two Spirits Attendant on Each Man, and How to Distinguish the Suggestions of the One from Those of the Other

CHAPTER I

"I gave you," he said, "directions in the first commandment to attend to faith, and fear, and self-restraint." "Even so, sir," said I. And he said, "Now I wish to show you the powers of these, that you may know what power each possesses. For their powers are double, and have relation alike to the righteous and the unrighteous. Trust you, therefore, the righteous, but put no trust in the unrighteous. For the path of righteousness is straight, but that of unrighteousness is crooked. But walk in the straight and even way, and mind not the crooked. For the crooked path has no roads, but has many pathless places and stumbling-blocks in it, and it is rough and thorny. It is injurious to those who walk therein. But they who walk in the straight road walk evenly without stumbling, because it is neither rough nor thorny. You see, then, that it is better to walk in this road." "I wish to go by this road," said I. "You will go by it," said he; "and whoever turns to the Lord with all his heart will walk in it."

CHAPTER II

"Hear now," said he, "in regard to faith. There are two angels with a man—one of righteousness, and the other of iniquity." And I said to him, "How, sir, am I to know the powers of these, for both angels dwell with me?" "Hear," said he, and "understand them. The angel of righteousness is gentle and modest, meek and peaceful. When, therefore, he ascends into your heart, forthwith he talks to you of righteousness, purity, chastity, contentment, and of every righteous deed and glorious virtue. When all these ascend into your heart, know that the angel of righteousness is with you. These are the deeds of the angel of righteousness. Trust him, then, and his works. Look now at the works of the angel of iniquity. First, he is wrathful, and bitter, and foolish, and his works are evil, and ruin the servants of God. When, then, he ascends into your heart, know him by his works." And I said to him, "How, sir, I shall perceive him, I do not know." "Hear and understand" said he. "When anger comes upon you, or harshness, know that he is in you; and you will know this to be the case also, when you are attacked by a longing after many transactions, and the richest delicacies, and drunken revels, and divers luxuries, and things improper, and by a hankering after women, and by overreaching, and pride, and blustering, and by whatever is like to these. When these ascend into your heart, know that the angel of iniquity is in you. Now that you know his works, depart from him, and in no respect trust him, because his deeds are evil, and unprofitable to the servants of God. These, then, are the actions of both angels. Understand them, and trust the angel of righteousness; but depart from the angel of iniquity, because his instruction is bad in every deed. For though a man be most faithful, and the thought of this angel ascend into his heart, that man or woman must sin. On the other hand, be a man or woman ever so bad, yet, if the works of the angel of righteousness ascend into his or her heart, he or she must do something good. You see, therefore, that it is good to follow the angel of righteousness, but to bid farewell to the angel of iniquity." "This commandment exhibits the deeds of faith, that you may trust the works of the angel of righteousness, and doing them you may live to God. But believe the works of the angel of iniquity are hard. If you refuse to do them, you will live to God."

Commandment Seventh

On Fearing God, and Not Fearing the Devil

"Fear," said he, "the Lord, and keep His commandments. For if you keep the commandments of God, you will be powerful in every action, and every one of your actions will be incomparable. For, fearing the Lord, you will do all things well. This is the fear which you ought to have, that you may be saved. But fear not the devil; for, fearing the Lord, you will have dominion over the devil, for there is no power in him. But he in whom there is no power ought on no account to be an object of fear; but He in whom there is glorious power is truly to be feared. For every one that has power ought to be feared; but he who has not power is despised by all. Fear, therefore, the deeds of the devil, since they are wicked. For, fearing the Lord, you will not do these deeds, but will refrain from them. For fears are of two kinds: for if you do not wish to do that which is evil, fear the Lord, and you will not do it; but, again, if you wish to do that which is good, fear the Lord, and you will do it. Wherefore the fear of the Lord is strong, and great, and glorious. Fear, then, the Lord, and you will live to Him, and as many as fear Him and keep His commandments will live to God." "Why," said I, "sir, did you say in regard to those that keep His commandments, that they will live to God?" "Because," says he, "all creation fears the Lord, but all creation does not keep His commandments. They only who fear the Lord and keep His commandments have life with God; but as to those who keep not His commandments, there is no life in them."

Commandment Eighth

We Ought to Shun that Which is Evil, and Do that Which is Good

"I told you," said he, "that the creatures of God are double, for restraint also is double; for in some cases restraint has to be exercised, in others there is no need of restraint." "Make known to me, sir," say I, "in what cases restraint has to be exercised, and in what cases it has not." "Restrain yourself in regard to evil, and do it not; but exercise no restraint in regard to good, but do it. For if you exercise restraint in the doing of good, you will commit a great sin; but if you exercise restraint, so as not to do that which is evil, you are practising great righteousness. Restrain yourself, therefore, from all iniquity, and do that which is good." "What, sir," say I, "are the evil deeds from which we must restrain ourselves?" "Hear," says he: "from adultery and fornication, from unlawful revelling, from wicked luxury, from indulgence in many kinds of food and the extravagance of riches, and from boastfulness, and haughtiness, and insolence, and lies, and backbiting, and hypocrisy, from the remembrance of wrong, and from all slander. These are the deeds that are most wicked in the life of men. From all these deeds, therefore, the servant of God must restrain himself. For he who does not restrain himself from these, cannot live to God. Listen, then, to the deeds that accompany these." "Are there, sir," said I, "any other evil deeds?" "There are," says he; "and many of them, too, from which the servant of God must restrain himself—theft, lying, robbery, false witness, overreaching, wicked lust, deceit, vainglory, boastfulness, and all other vices like to these." "Do you not think that these are really wicked?" "Exceedingly wicked in the servants of God. From all of these the servant of God must restrain himself. Restrain yourself, then, from all these, that you may live to God, and you will be enrolled amongst those who restrain themselves in regard to these matters. These, then, are the things from which you must restrain yourself."

"But listen," says he, "to the things in regard to which you have not to exercise self-restraint, but which you ought to do. Restrain not yourself in regard to that which is good, but do it." "And tell me, sir," say I, "the nature of the good deeds, that I may walk in them and wait on them, so that doing them I can be saved." "Listen," says he, "to the good deeds which you ought to do, and in regard to which there is no self-restraint requisite. First of all there is faith, then fear of the Lord, love, concord, words of righteousness, truth, patience. Than these, nothing is better in the life of men. If any one attend to these, and restrain himself not from them, blessed is he in his life. Then there are the following attendant on these: helping widows, looking after orphans and the needy, rescuing the servants of God from necessities, the being hospitable—for in hospitality good-doing finds a field—never opposing any one, the being quiet, having fewer needs than all men, reverencing the aged, practising righteousness, watching the brotherhood, bearing insolence, being long-suffering, encouraging those who are sick in soul, not casting those who have fallen into sin from the faith, but turning them back and restoring them to peace of mind, admonishing sinners, not oppressing debtors and the needy, and if there are any other actions like these. Do these seem to you good?" says he. "For what, sir," say I, "is better than these?" "Walk then in them," says he, "and restrain not yourself from them, and you will live to God. Keep, therefore, this commandment. If you do good, and restrain not yourself from it, you will live to God. All who act thus will live to God. And, again, if you refuse to do evil, and restrain yourself from it, you will live to God. And all will live to God who keep these commandments, and walk in them."

Commandment Ninth

Prayer Must Be Made to God Without Ceasing, and with Unwavering Confidence

He says to me, "Put away doubting from you and do not hesitate to ask of the Lord, saying to yourself, 'How can I ask of the Lord and receive from Him, seeing I have sinned so much against Him? 'Do not thus reason with yourself, but with all your heart turn to the Lord and ask of Him without doubting, and you will know the multitude of His tender mercies; that He will never leave you, but fulfil the request of your soul. For He is not like men, who remember evils done against them; but He Himself remembers not evils, and has compassion on His own creature. Cleanse, therefore, your heart from all the vanities of this world, and from the words already mentioned, and ask of the Lord and you will receive all, and in none of your requests will you be denied which you make to the Lord without doubting. But if you doubt in your heart, you will receive none of your requests. For those who doubt regarding God are double-souled, and obtain not one of their requests. But those who are perfect in faith ask everything, trusting in the Lord; and they obtain, because they ask nothing doubting, and not being double-souled. For every double-souled man, even if he repent, will with difficulty be saved. Cleanse your heart, therefore, from all doubt, and put on faith, because it is strong, and trust God that you will obtain from Him all that you ask. And if at any time, after you have asked of the Lord, you are slower in obtaining your request [than you expected], do not doubt because you have not soon obtained the request of your soul; for invariably it is on account of some temptation or some sin of which you are ignorant that you are slower in obtaining your request. Wherefore do not cease to make the request of your soul, and you will obtain it. But if you grow weary and waver in your request, blame yourself, and not Him who does not give to you. Consider this doubting state of mind, for it is wicked and senseless, and turns many away entirely from the faith, even though they be very strong. For this doubting is the daughter of the devil, and acts exceedingly wickedly to the servants of God. Despise, then, doubting, and gain the mastery over it in everything; clothing yourself with faith, which is strong and powerful. For faith promises all things, perfects all things; but doubt having no thorough faith in itself, fails in every work which it undertakes. You see, then," says he, "that, faith is from above—from the Lord—and has great power; but doubt is an earthly spirit, coming from the devil, and has no power. Serve, then, that which has power, namely faith, and keep away from doubt, which has no power, and you will live to God. And all will live to God whose minds have been set on these things."

Commandment Tenth

Of Grief, and Not Grieving the Spirit of God Which is in Us

CHAPTER I

"Remove from you," says he, "grief; for she is the sister of doubt and anger." "How, sir," say I, "is she the sister of these? for anger, doubt, and grief seem to be quite different from each other." "You are senseless, O man. Do you not perceive that grief is more wicked than all the spirits, and most terrible to the servants of God, and more than all other spirits destroys man and crushes out the Holy Spirit, and yet, on the other hand, she saves him?" "I am senseless, sir," say I, "and do not understand these parables. For how she can crush out, and on the other hand save, I do not perceive." "Listen," says he. "Those who have never searched for the truth, nor investigated the nature of the Divinity, but have simply believed, when they devote themselves to and become mixed up with business, and wealth, and heathen friendships, and many other actions of this world, do not perceive the parables of Divinity; for their minds are darkened by these actions, and they are corrupted and become dried up. Even as beautiful vines, when they are neglected, are withered up by thorns and divers plants, so men who have believed, and have afterwards fallen away into many of those actions above mentioned, go astray in their minds, and lose all understanding in regard to righteousness; for if they hear of righteousness, their minds are occupied with their business, and they give no heed at all. Those, on the other hand, who have the fear of God, and search after Godhead and truth, and have their hearts turned to the Lord, quickly perceive and understand what is said to them, because they have the fear of the Lord in them. For where the Lord dwells, there is much understanding. Cleave, then, to the Lord, and you will understand and perceive all things."

CHAPTER II

"Hear, then," says he, "foolish man, how grief crushes out the Holy Spirit, and on the other hand saves. When the doubting man attempts any deed, and fails in it on account of his doubt, this grief enters into the man, and grieves the Holy Spirit, and crushes him out. Then, on the other hand, when anger attaches itself to a man in regard to any matter, and he is embittered, then grief enters into the heart of the man who was irritated, and he is grieved at the deed which he did, and repents that he has wrought a wicked deed. This grief, then, appears to be accompanied by salvation, because the man, after having done a wicked deed, repented. Both actions grieve the Spirit: doubt, because it did not accomplish its object; and anger grieves the Spirit, because it did what was wicked. Both these are grievous to the Holy Spirit—doubt and anger. Wherefore remove grief from you, and crush not the Holy Spirit which dwells in you, lest he entreat God against you, and he withdraw from you. For the Spirit of God which has been granted to us to dwell in this body does not endure grief nor straitness. Wherefore put on cheerfulness, which always is agreeable and acceptable to God, and rejoice in it. For every cheerful man does what is good, and minds what is good, and despises grief; but the sorrowful man always acts wickedly. First, he acts wickedly because he grieves the Holy Spirit, which was given to man a cheerful Spirit. Secondly, Grieving the Holy Spirit, he works iniquity, neither entreating the Lord nor confessing to Him. For the entreaty of the sorrowful man has no power to ascend to the altar of God." "Why," say I, "does not the entreaty of the grieved man ascend to the altar?" "Because," says he, "grief sits in his heart. Grief, then, mingled with his entreaty, does not permit the entreaty to ascend pure to the altar of God. For as vinegar and wine, when mixed in the same vessel, do not give the same pleasure [as wine alone gives], so grief mixed with the Holy Spirit does not produce the same entreaty [as would be produced by the Holy Spirit alone]. Cleanse yourself from this wicked grief, and you will live to God; and all will live to God who drive away grief from them, and put on all cheerfulness."

Commandment Eleventh

The Spirit and Prophets to Be Tried by Their Works; Also of the Two Kinds of Spirit

He pointed out to me some men sitting on a seat, and one man sitting on a chair. And he says to me, "Do you see the persons sitting on the seat?" "I do, sir," said I. "These," says he, "are the faithful, and he who sits on the chair is a false prophet, ruining the minds of the servants of God. It is the doubters, not the faithful, that he ruins. These doubters then go to him as to a soothsayer, and inquire of him what will happen to them; and he, the false prophet, not having the power of a Divine Spirit in him, answers them according to their inquiries, and according to their wicked desires, and fills their souls with expectations, according to their own wishes. For being himself empty, he gives empty answers to empty inquirers; for every answer is made to the emptiness of man. Some true words he does occasionally utter; for the devil fills him with his own spirit, in the hope that he may be able to overcome some of the righteous. As many, then, as are strong in the faith of the Lord, and are clothed with truth, have no connection with such spirits, but keep away from them; but as many as are of doubtful minds and frequently repent, betake themselves to soothsaying, even as the heathen, and bring greater sin upon themselves by their idolatry. For he who inquires of a false prophet in regard to any action is an idolater, and devoid of the truth, and foolish. For no spirit given by God requires to be asked; but such a spirit having the power of Divinity speaks all things of itself, for it proceeds from above from the power of the Divine Spirit. But the spirit which is asked and speaks according to the desires of men is earthly, light, and powerless, and it is altogether silent if it is not questioned." "How then, sir," say I, "will a man know which of them is the prophet, and which the false prophet?" "I will tell you," says he, "about both the prophets, and then you can try the true and the false prophet according to my directions. Try the man who has the Divine Spirit by his life. First, he who has the Divine Spirit proceeding from above is meek, and peaceable, and humble, and refrains from all iniquity and the vain desire of this world, and contents himself with fewer wants than those of other men, and when asked he makes no reply; nor does he speak privately, nor when man wishes the spirit to speak does the Holy

Spirit speak, but it speaks only when God wishes it to speak. When, then, a man having the Divine Spirit comes into an assembly of righteous men who have faith in the Divine Spirit, and this assembly of men offers up prayer to God, then the angel of the prophetic Spirit, who is destined for him, fills the man; and the man being filled with the Holy Spirit, speaks to the multitude as the Lord wishes. Thus, then, will the Spirit of Divinity become manifest. Whatever power therefore comes from the Spirit of Divinity belongs to the Lord. Hear, then," says he, "in regard to the spirit which is earthly, and empty, and powerless, and foolish. First, the man who seems to have the Spirit exalts himself, and wishes to have the first seat, and is bold, and impudent, and talkative, and lives in the midst of many luxuries and many other delusions, and takes rewards for his prophecy; and if he does not receive rewards, he does not prophesy. Can, then, the Divine Spirit take rewards and prophesy? It is not possible that the prophet of God should do this, but prophets of this character are possessed by an earthly spirit. Then it never approaches an assembly of righteous men, but shuns them. And it associates with doubters and the vain, and prophesies to them in a corner, and deceives them, speaking to them, according to their desires, mere empty words: for they are empty to whom it gives its answers. For the empty vessel, when placed along with the empty, is not crushed, but they correspond to each other. When, therefore, it comes into an assembly of righteous men who have a Spirit of Divinity, and they offer up prayer, that man is made empty, and the earthly spirit tees from him through fear, and that man is made dumb, and is entirely crushed, being unable to speak. For if you pack closely a storehouse with wine or oil, and put an empty jar in the midst of the vessels of wine or oil, you will find that jar empty as when you placed it, if you should wish to clear the storehouse. So also the empty prophets, when they come to the spirits of the righteous, are found [on leaving] to be such as they were when they came. This, then, is the mode of life of both prophets. Try by his deeds and his life the man who says that he is inspired. But as for you, trust the Spirit which comes from God, and has power; but the spirit which is earthly and empty trust not at all, for there is no power in it: it comes from the devil. Hear, then, the parable which I am to tell you. Take a stone, and throw it to the sky, and see if you can touch it. Or again, take a squirt of water and squirt into the sky, and see if you can penetrate the sky." "How, sir," say I, "can these things take place? for both of them are impossible." "As these things," says he, "are impossible, so also are the earthly spirits powerless and pithless. But look, on the other hand, at the power which comes from above. Hail is of the size of a very small grain, yet when it falls on a man's head how much annoyance it gives him! Or, again, take the drop which falls from a pitcher to the ground, and yet it hollows a stone. You see, then, that the smallest things coming from above have great power when they fall upon the earth. Thus also is the Divine Spirit, which comes from above, powerful. Trust, then, that Spirit, but have nothing to do with the other."

Commandment Twelfth

On the Twofold Desire. The Commandments of God Can Be Kept, and Believers Ought Not to Fear the Devil

CHAPTER I

He says to me, "Put away from you all wicked desire, and clothe yourself with good and chaste desire; for clothed with this desire you will hate wicked desire, and will rein yourself in even as you wish. For wicked desire is wild, and is with difficulty tamed. For it is terrible, and consumes men exceedingly by its wildness. Especially is the servant of God terribly consumed by it, if he falls into it and is devoid of understanding. Moreover, it consumes all such as have not on them the garment of good desire, but are entangled and mixed up with this world. These it delivers up to death." "What then, sir," say I, "are the deeds of wicked desire which deliver men over to death? Make them known to me, and I will refrain from them." "Listen, then, to the works in which evil desire slays the servants of God."

CHAPTER II

"Foremost of all is the desire after another's wife or husband, and after extravagance, and many useless dainties and drinks, and many other foolish luxuries; for all luxury is foolish and empty in the servants of God. These, then, are the evil desires which slay the servants of God. For this evil desire is the daughter of the devil. You must refrain from evil desires, that by refraining ye may live to God. But as many as are mastered by them, and do not resist them, will perish at last, for these desires are fatal. Put you on, then, the desire of righteousness; and arming yourself with the fear of the Lord, resist them. For the fear of the Lord dwells in good desire. But if evil desire see you armed with the fear of God, and resisting it, it will flee far from you, and it will no longer appear to you, for it fears your armour. Go, then, garlanded with the crown which you have gained for victory over it, to the desire of righteousness, and, delivering up to it the prize which you have received, serve it even as it wishes. If you serve good desire, and be subject to it, you will gain the mastery over evil desire, and make it subject to you even as you wish."

CHAPTER III

"I should like to know," say I, "in what way I ought to serve good desire." "Hear," says he: "You will practice righteousness and virtue, truth and the fear of the Lord, faith and meekness, and whatsoever excellences are like to these. Practising these, you will be a well-pleasing servant of God, and you will live to Him; and every one who shall serve good desire, shall live to God."

He concluded the twelve commandments, and said to me, "You have now these commandments. Walk in them, and exhort your hearers that their repentance may be pure during the remainder of their life. Fulfil carefully this ministry which I now entrust to you, and you will accomplish much. For you will find favour among those who are to repent, and they will give heed to your words; for I will be with you, and will compel them to obey you." I say to him, "Sir, these commandments are great, and good, and glorious, and fitted to gladden the heart of the man who can perform them. But I do not know if these commandments can be kept by man, because they are exceeding hard." He answered and said to me, "If you lay it down as certain that they can be kept, then you will easily keep them, and they will not be hard. But if you come to imagine that they cannot be kept by man, then you will not keep them. Now I say to you, If you do not keep them, but neglect them, you will not be saved, nor your children, nor your house, since you have already determined for yourself that these commandments cannot be kept by man."

CHAPTER IV

These things he said to me in tones of the deepest anger, so that I was confounded and exceedingly afraid of him, for his figure was altered so that a man could not endure his anger. But seeing me altogether agitated and confused, he began to speak to me in more gentle tones; and he said: "O fool, senseless and doubting, do you not perceive how great is the glory of God, and how strong and marvellous, in that He created the world for the sake of man, and subjected all creation to him, and gave him power to rule over everything under heaven? If, then, man is lord of the creatures of God, and rules over all, is he not able to be lord also of these commandments? For," says he, "the man who has the Lord in his heart can also be lord of all, and of every one of these commandments. But to those who have the Lord only on their lips, but their hearts hardened, and who are far from the Lord, the commandments are hard and difficult. Put, therefore, ye who are empty and fickle in your faith, the Lord in your heart, and ye will know that there is nothing easier or sweeter, or more manageable, than these commandments. Return, ye who walk in the commandments of the devil, in hard, and bitter, and wild licentiousness, and fear not the devil; for there is no power in him against you, for I will be with you, the angel of repentance, who am lord over him. The devil has fear only, but his fear has no strength. Fear him not, then, and he will flee from you."

CHAPTER V

I say to him, "Sir, listen to me for a moment." "Say what you wish," says he. "Man, sir," say I, "is eager to keep the commandments of God, and there is no one who does not ask of the Lord that strength may be given him for these commandments, and that he may be subject to them; but the devil is hard, and holds sway over them." "He cannot," says he, "hold sway over the servants of God, who with all their heart place their hopes in Him. The devil can wrestle against these, overthrow them he cannot. If, then, ye resist him, he will be conquered, and flee in disgrace from you. As many, therefore," says he, "as are empty, fear the devil, as possessing power. When a man has filled very suitable jars with good wine, and a few among those jars are left empty, then he comes to the jars, and does not look at the full jars, for he knows that they are full; but he looks at the empty, being afraid lest they have become sour. For empty jars quickly become sour, and the goodness of the wine is gone. So also the devil goes to all the servants of God to try them. As many, then, as are full in the faith, resist him strongly, and he withdraws from them, having no way by which he might enter them. He goes, then, to the empty, and finding a way of entrance, into them, he produces in them whatever he wishes, and they become his servants."

CHAPTER VI

"But I, the angel of repentance, say to you Fear not the devil; for I was sent," says he, "to be with you who repent with all your heart, and to make you strong in faith. Trust God, then, ye who on account of your sins have despaired of life, and who add to your sins and weigh down your life; for if ye return to the Lord with all your heart, and practice righteousness the rest of your days, and serve Him according to His will, He will heal your former sins, and you will have power to hold sway over the works of the devil. But as to the threats of the devil, fear them not at all, for he is powerless as the sinews of a dead man. Give ear to me, then, and fear Him who has all power, both to save and destroy, and keep His commandments, and ye will live to God." I say to him, "Sir, I am now made strong in all the ordinances of the Lord, because you are with me; and I know that you will crush all the power of the devil, and we shall have rule over him, and shall prevail against all his works. And I hope, sir, to be able to keep all these commandments which you have enjoined upon me, the Lord strengthening me." "You will keep them," says he, "if your heart be pure towards the Lord; and all will keep them who cleanse their hearts from the vain desires of this world, and they will live to God."

Book of Similitudes

Similitude First

As in This World We Have No Abiding City, We Ought to Seek One to Come

He says to me, "You know that you who are the servants of God dwell in a strange land; for your city is far away from this one. If, then," he continues, "you know your city in which you are to dwell, why do ye here provide lands, and make expensive preparations, and accumulate dwellings and useless buildings? He who makes such preparations for this city cannot return again to his own. Oh foolish, and unstable, and miserable man! Dost thou not understand that all these things belong to another, and are under the power of another? for the lord of this city will say, 'I do not wish thee to dwell in my city; but depart from this city, because thou obeyest not my laws.' Thou, therefore, although having fields and houses, and many other things, when cast out by him, what wilt thou do with thy land, and house, and other possessions which thou hast gathered to thyself? For the lord of this country justly says to thee, 'Either obey my laws or depart from my dominion.' What, then, dost thou intend to do, having a law in thine own city, on account of thy lands, and the rest of thy possessions? Thou shalt altogether deny thy law, and walk according to the law of this city. See lest it be to thy hurt to deny thy law; for if thou shalt desire to return to thy city, thou wilt not be received, because thou hast denied the law of thy city, but wilt be excluded from it. Have a care, therefore: as one living in a foreign land, make no further preparations for thyself than such merely as may be sufficient; and be ready, when the master of this city shall come to cast thee out for disobeying his law, to leave his city, and to depart to thine own, and to obey thine own law without being exposed to annoyance, but in great joy. Have a care, then, ye who serve the Lord, and have Him in your heart, that ye work the works of God, remembering His commandments and promises which He promised, and believe that He will bring them to pass if His commandments be observed. Instead of lands, therefore, buy afflicted souls, according as each one is able, and visit widows and orphans, and do not overlook them; and spend your wealth and all your preparations, which ye received from the Lord, upon such lands and houses. For to this end did the Master make you rich, that you might perform these services unto Him; and it is much better to purchase such lands, and possessions, and houses, as you will find in your own city, when you come to reside in it. This is a noble and sacred expenditure, attended neither with sorrow nor fear, but with joy. Do not practice the expenditure of the heathen, for it is injurious to you who are the servants of God; but practice an expenditure of your own, in which ye can rejoice; and do not corrupt nor touch what is another's nor covet it, for it is an evil thing to covet the goods of other men; but work thine own work, and thou wilt be saved."

Similitude Second

As the Vine is Supported by the Elm, So is the Rich Man Helped by the Prayer of the Poor

As I was walking in the field, and observing an elm and vine, and determining in my own mind respecting them and their fruits, the Shepherd appears to me, and says, "What is it that you are thinking about the elm and vine?" "I am considering," I reply, "that they become each other exceedingly well." "These two trees," he continues, "are intended as an example for the servants of God." "I would like to know," said I, "the example which these trees you say, are intended to teach." "Do you see," he says, "the elm and the vine?" "I see them sir," I replied. "This vine," he continued, "produces fruit, and the elm is an unfruitful tree; but unless the vine be trained upon the elm, it cannot bear much fruit when extended at length upon the ground; and the fruit which it does bear is rotten, because the plant is not suspended upon the elm. When, therefore, the vine is cast upon the elm, it yields fruit both from itself and from the elm. You see, moreover, that the elm also produces much fruit, not less than the vine, but even more; because," he continued, "the vine, when suspended upon the elm, yields much fruit, and good; but when thrown upon the ground, what it produces is small and rotten. This similitude, therefore, is for the servants of God—for the poor man and for the rich." "How so, sir?" said I; "explain the matter to me." "Listen," he said: "The rich man has much wealth, but is poor in matters relating to the Lord, because he is distracted about his riches; and he offers very few confessions and intercessions to the Lord, and those which he does offer are small and weak, and have no power above. But when the rich man refreshes the poor, and assists him in his necessities, believing that what he does to the poor man will be able to find its reward with God—because the poor man is rich in intercession and confession, and his intercession has great power with God—then the rich man helps the poor in all things without hesitation; and the poor man, being helped by the rich, intercedes for him, giving thanks to God for him who bestows gifts upon him. And he still continues to interest himself zealously for the poor man, that his wants may be constantly supplied. For he knows that the intercession of the poor man is acceptable and influential with God. Both, accordingly, accomplish their work. The poor man makes intercession; a work in which he is rich, which he received from the Lord, and with which he recompenses the master who helps him. And the rich man, in like manner, unhesitatingly bestows upon the poor man the riches which he received from the Lord. And this is a great work, and acceptable before God, because he understands the object of his wealth, and has given to the poor of the gifts of the Lord, and rightly discharged his service to Him. Among men, however, the elm appears not to produce fruit, and they do not know nor understand that if a drought come, the elm, which contains water, nourishes the vine; and the vine, having an unfailing supply of water, yields double fruit both for itself and for the elm. So also poor men interceding with the Lord on behalf of the rich, increase their riches; and the rich, again, aiding the poor in their necessities, satisfy their souls. Both, therefore, are partners in the righteous work. He who does these things shall not be deserted by God, but shall be enrolled in the books of the living. Blessed are they who have riches, and who understand that they are from the Lord. [For they who are of that mind will be able to do some good.]"

Similitude Third

As in Winter Green Trees Cannot Be Distinguished from Withered, So in This World Neither Can the Just from the Unjust

He showed me many trees having no leaves, but withered, as it seemed to me; for all were alike. And he said to me, "Do you see those trees?" "I see, sir," I replied, "that all are alike, and withered." He answered me, and said, "These trees which you see are those who dwell in this world." "Why, then, sir," I said, "are they withered, as it were, and alike?" "Because," he said, "neither are the righteous manifest in this life, nor sinners, but they are alike; for this life is a winter to the righteous, and they do not manifest themselves, because they dwell with sinners: for as in winter trees that have cast their leaves are alike, and it is not seen which are dead and which are living, so in this world neither do the righteous show themselves, nor sinners, but all are alike one to another."

Similitude Fourth

As in Summer Living Trees are Distinguished from Withered by Fruit and Living Leaves, So in the World to Come the Just Differ from the Unjust in Happiness

He showed me again many trees, some budding, and others withered. And he said to me, "Do you see these trees?" "I see, sir," I replied, "some putting forth buds, and others withered." "Those," he said, "which are budding are the righteous who are to live in the world to come; for the coming world is the summer of the righteous, but the winter of sinners. When, therefore, the mercy of the Lord shines forth, then shall they be made manifest who are the servants of God, and all men shall be made manifest. For as in summer the fruits of each individual tree appear, and it is ascertained of what sort they are, so also the fruits of the righteous shall be manifest, and all who have been fruitful in that world shall be made known. But the heathen and sinners, like the withered trees which you saw, will be found to be those who have been withered and unfruitful in that world, and shall be burnt as wood, and [so] made manifest, because their actions were evil during their lives. For the sinners shall be consumed because they sinned and did not repent, and the heathen shall be burned because they knew not Him who created them. Do you therefore bear fruit, that in that summer your fruit may be known. And refrain from much business, and you will never sin: for they who are occupied with much business commit also many sins, being distracted about their affairs, and not at all serving their Lord. How, then," he continued, "can such a one ask and obtain anything from the Lord, if he serve Him not? They who serve Him shall obtain their requests, but they who serve Him not shall receive nothing. And in the performance even of a single action a man can serve the Lord; for his mind will not be perverted from the Lord, but he will serve Him, having a pure mind. If, therefore, you do these things, you shall be able to bear fruit for the life to come. And every one who will do these things shall bear fruit."

Similitude Fifth

Of True Fasting and Its Reward: Also of Purity of Body

CHAPTER I

While fasting and sitting on a certain mountain, and giving thanks to the Lord for all His dealings with me, I see the Shepherd sitting down beside me, and saying, "Why have you come hither [so] early in the morning?" "Because, sir," I answered, "I have a station." "What is a station?" he asked. "I am fasting, sir," I replied. "What is this fasting," he continued, "which you are observing?" "As

I have been accustomed, sir," I reply, "so I fast." "You do not know," he says, "how to fast unto the Lord: this useless fasting which you observe to Him is of no value." "Why, sir," I answered, "do you say this?" "I say to you," he continued, "that the fasting which you think you observe is not a fasting. But I will teach you what is a full and acceptable fasting to the Lord. Listen," he continued: "God does not desire such an empty fasting. For fasting to God in this way you will do nothing for a righteous life; but offer to God a fasting of the following kind: Do no evil in your life, and serve the Lord with a pure heart: keep His commandments, walking in His precepts, and let no evil desire arise in your heart; and believe in God. If you do these things, and fear Him, and abstain from every evil thing, you will live unto God; and if you do these things, you will keep a great fast, and one acceptable before God."

CHAPTER II

"Hear the similitude which I am about to narrate to you relative to fasting. A certain man had a field and many slaves, and he planted a certain part of the field with a vineyard, and selecting a faithful and beloved and much valued slave, he called him to him, and said, 'Take this vineyard which I have planted, and stake it until I come, and do nothing else to the vineyard; and attend to this order of mine, and you shall receive your freedom from me.' And the master of the slave departed to a foreign country. And when he was gone, the slave took and staked the vineyard; and when he had finished the staking of the vines, he saw that the vineyard was full of weeds. He then reflected, saying, 'I have kept this order of my master: I will dig up the rest of this vineyard, and it will be more beautiful when dug up; and being free of weeds, it will yield more fruit, not being choked by them.' He took, therefore, and dug up the vineyard, and rooted out all the weeds that were in it. And that vineyard became very beautiful and fruitful, having no weeds to choke it. And after a certain time the master of the slave and of the field returned, and entered into the vineyard. And seeing that the vines were suitably supported on stakes, and the ground, moreover, dug up, and all the weeds rooted out, and the vines fruitful, he was greatly pleased with the work of his slave. And calling his beloved son who was his heir, and his friends who were his councillors, he told them what orders he had given his slave, and what he had found performed. And they rejoiced along with the slave at the testimony which his master bore to him. And he said to them, 'I promised this slave freedom if he obeyed the command which I gave him; and he has kept my command, and done besides a good work to the vineyard, and has pleased me exceedingly. In return, therefore, for the work which he has done, I wish to make him co-heir with my son, because, having good thoughts, he did not neglect them, but carried them out.' With this resolution of the master his son and friends were well pleased, viz., that the slave should be co-heir with the son. After a few days the master made a feast, and sent to his slave many dishes from his table. And the slave receiving the dishes that were sent him from his master, took of them what was sufficient for himself, and distributed the rest among his fellow-slaves. And his fellow-slaves rejoiced to receive the dishes, and began to pray for him, that he might find still greater favour with his master for having so treated them. His master heard all these things that were done, and was again greatly pleased with his conduct. And the master again calling together his friends and his son, reported to them the slave's proceeding with regard to the dishes which he had sent him. And they were still more satisfied that the slave should become co-heir with his son."

CHAPTER III

I said to him, "Sir, I do not see the meaning of these similitudes, nor am I able to comprehend them, unless you explain them to me." "I will explain them all to you," he said, "and whatever I shall mention in the course of our conversations I will show you. [Keep the commandments of the Lord, and you will be approved, and inscribed amongst the number of those who observe His commands.] And if you do any good beyond what is commanded by God, you will gain for yourself more abundant glory, and will be more honoured by God than you would otherwise be. If, therefore, in keeping the commandments of God, you do, in addition, these services, you will have joy if you observe them according to my command." I said to him, "Sir, whatsoever you enjoin upon me I will observe, for I know that you are with me." "I will be with you," he replied, "because you have such a desire for doing good; and I will be with all those," he added, "who have such a desire. This fasting," he continued, "is very good, provided the commandments of the Lord be observed. Thus, then, shall you observe the fasting which you intend to keep. First of all, be on your guard against every evil word, and every evil desire, and purify your heart from all the vanities of this world. If you guard against these things, your fasting will be perfect. And you will do also as follows. Having fulfilled what is written, in the day on which you fast you will taste nothing but bread and water; and having reckoned up the price of the dishes of that day which you intended to have eaten, you will give it to a widow, or an orphan, or to some person in want, and thus you will exhibit humility of mind, so that he who has received benefit from your humility may fill his own soul, and pray for you to the Lord. If you observe fasting, as I have commanded you, your sacrifice will be acceptable to God, and this fasting will be written down; and the service thus performed is noble, and sacred, and acceptable to the Lord. These things, therefore, shall you thus observe with your children, and all your house, and in observing them you will be blessed; and as many as hear these words and observe them shall be blessed; and whatsoever they ask of the Lord they shall receive."

CHAPTER IV

I prayed him much that he would explain to me the similitude of the field, and of the master of the vineyard, and of the slave who staked the vineyard, and of the sakes, and of the weeds that were plucked out of the vineyard, and of the son, and of the friends who were fellow-councillors, for I knew that all these things were a kind of parable. And he answered me, and said, "You are exceedingly persistent with your questions. You ought not," he continued, "to ask any questions at all; for if it is needful to explain anything, it will be made known to you." I said to him, "Sir, whatsoever you show me, and do not explain, I shall have seen to no purpose, not understanding its meaning. In like manner, also, if you speak parables to me, and do not unfold them, I shall have heard your words in vain." And he answered me again, saying, "Every one who is the servant of God, and has his Lord in his heart, asks of Him understanding, and receives it, and opens up every parable; and the words of the Lord become known to him which are spoken in parables. But those who are weak and slothful in prayer, hesitate to ask anything from the Lord; but the Lord is full of compassion, and gives without fail to all who ask Him. But you, having been strengthened by the holy Angel, and having obtained from Him such intercession, and not being slothful, why do not you ask of the Lord understanding, and receive it from Him?" I said to him, "Sir, having you with me, I am necessitated to ask questions of you, for you show me all things, and converse with me; but if I were to see or hear these things without you, I would then ask the Lord to explain them."

CHAPTER V

"I said to you a little ago," he answered, "that you were cunning and obstinate in asking explanations of the parables; but since you are so persistent, I shall unfold to you the meaning of the similitudes of the field, and of all the others that follow, that you may make them known to every one. Hear now," he said, "and understand them. The field is this world; and the Lord of the field is He who created, and perfected, and strengthened all things; [and the son is the Holy Spirit;] and the slave is the Son of God; and the vines are this people, whom He Himself planted; and the stakes are the holy angels of the Lord, who keep His people together; and the weeds that were plucked out of the vineyard are the iniquities of God's servants; and the dishes which He sent Him from His table are the commandments which He gave His people through His Son; and the friends and fellow-councillors are the holy angels who were first created; and the Master's absence from home is the time that remains until His appearing." I said to him, "Sir, all these are great, and marvellous, and glorious things. Could I, therefore," I continued, "understand them? No, nor could any other man, even if exceedingly wise. Moreover," I added, "explain to me what I am about to ask you." "Say what you wish," he replied. "Why, sir," I asked, "is the Son of God in the parable in the form of a slave?"

CHAPTER VI

"Hear," he answered: "the Son of God is not in the form of a slave, but in great power and might." "How so, sir?" I said; "I do not understand." "Because," he answered, "God planted the vineyard, that is to say, He created the people, and gave them to His Son; and the Son appointed His angels over them to keep them; and He Himself purged away their sins, having suffered many trials and undergone many labours, for no one is able to dig without labour and toil. He Himself, then, having purged away the sins of the people, showed them the paths of life by giving them the law which He received from His Father. [You see," he said, "that He is the Lord of the people, having received all authority from His Father.] And why the Lord took His Son as councillor, and the glorious angels, regarding the heirship of the slave, listen. The holy, pre-existent Spirit, that created every creature, God made to dwell in flesh, which He chose. This flesh, accordingly, in which the Holy Spirit dwelt, was nobly subject to that Spirit, walking religiously and chastely, in no respect defiling the Spirit; and accordingly, after living excellently and purely, and after labouring and co-operating with the Spirit, and having in everything acted vigorously and courageously along with the Holy Spirit, He assumed it as a partner with it. For this conduct of the flesh pleased Him, because it was not defiled on the earth while having the Holy Spirit. He took, therefore, as fellow-councillors His Son and the glorious angels, in order that this flesh, which had been subject to the body without a fault, might have some place of tabernacle, and that it might not appear that the reward [of its servitude had been lost], for the flesh that has been found without spot or defilement, in which the Holy Spirit dwelt, [will receive a reward]. You have now the explanation of this parable also."

CHAPTER VII

"I rejoice, sir," I said, "to hear this explanation." "Hear," again he replied: "Keep this flesh pure and stainless, that the Spirit which inhabits it may bear witness to it, and your flesh may be justified. See that the thought never arise in your mind that this flesh of yours is corruptible, and you misuse it by any act of defilement. If you defile your flesh, you will also defile the Holy Spirit; and if you defile your flesh [and spirit], you will not live." "And if any one, sir," I said, "has been hitherto ignorant, before he heard these words, how can such a man be saved who has defiled his flesh?" "Respecting former sins of ignorance," he said, "God alone is able to heal them, for to Him belongs all power. [But be on your guard now, and the all-powerful and compassionate God will heal former transgressions], if for the time to come you defile not your body nor your spirit; for both are common, and cannot be defiled, the one without the other: keep both therefore pure, and you will live unto God."

Similitude Sixth

Of the Two Classes of Voluptuous Men, and of Their Death, Falling Away, and the Duration of Their Punishment

CHAPTER I

Sitting in my house, and glorifying the Lord for all that I had seen, and reflecting on the commandments, that they are excellent, and powerful, and glorious, and able to save a man's soul, I said within myself, "I shall be blessed if I walk in these commandments, and every one who walks in them will be blessed." While I was saying these words to myself, I suddenly see him sitting beside me, and hear him thus speak: "Why are you in doubt about the commandments which I gave you? They are excellent: have no doubt about them at all, but put on faith in the Lord, and you will walk in them, for I will strengthen you in them. These commandments are beneficial to those who intend to repent: for if they do not walk in them, their repentance is in vain. You, therefore, who repent cast away the wickedness of this world which wears you out; and by putting on all the virtues of a holy life, you will be able to keep these commandments, and will no longer add to the number of your sins. Walk, therefore, in these commandments of mine, and you will live unto God. All these things have been spoken to you by me." And after he had uttered these words, he said to me, "Let us go into the fields, and I will show you the shepherds of the flocks." "Let us go, sir," I replied. And we came to a certain plain, and he showed me a young man, a shepherd, clothed in a suit of garments of a yellow colour: and he was herding very many sheep, and these sheep were feeding luxuriously, as it were, and riotously, and merrily skipping hither and thither. The shepherd himself was merry, because of his flock; and the appearance of the shepherd was joyous, and he was running about amongst his flock. [And other sheep I saw rioting and luxuriating in one place, but not, however, leaping about.]

CHAPTER II

And he said to me, "Do you see this shepherd?" "I see him, sir," I said. "This," he answered, "is the angel of luxury and deceit:

he wears out the souls of the servants of God, and perverts them from the truth, deceiving them with wicked desires, through which they will perish; for they forget the commandments of the living God, and walk in deceits and empty luxuries; and they are ruined by the angel, some being brought to death, others to corruption." I said to him, "Sir, I do not know the meaning of these words, 'to death, and to corruption.'" "Listen," he said. "The sheep which you saw merry and leaping about, are those which have torn themselves away from God for ever, and have delivered themselves over to luxuries and deceits [of this world. Among them there is no return to life through repentance, because they have added to their other sins, and blasphemed the name of the Lord. Such men therefore, are appointed unto death. And the sheep which you saw not leaping, but feeding in one place, are they who have delivered themselves over to luxury and deceit], but have committed no blasphemy against the Lord. These have been perverted from the truth: among them there is the hope of repentance, by which it is possible to live. Corruption, then, has a hope of a kind of renewal, but death has everlasting ruin." Again I went forward a little way, and he showed me a tall shepherd, somewhat savage in his appearance, clothed in a white goatskin, and having a wallet on his shoulders, and a very hard staff with branches, and a large whip. And he had a very sour look, so that I was afraid of him, so forbidding was his aspect. This shepherd, accordingly, was receiving the sheep from the young shepherd, those, viz., that were rioting and luxuriating, but not leaping; and he cast them into a precipitous place, full of thistles and thorns, so that it was impossible to extricate the sheep from the thorns and thistles; but they were completely entangled amongst them. These, accordingly, thus entangled, pastured amongst the thorns and thistles, and were exceedingly miserable, being beaten by him; and he drove them hither and thither, and gave them no rest; and, altogether, these sheep were in a wretched plight.

CHAPTER III

Seeing them, therefore, so beaten and so badly used, I was grieved for them, because they were so tormented, and had no rest at all. And I said to the Shepherd who talked with me, "Sir, who is this shepherd, who is so pitiless and severe, and so completely devoid of compassion for these sheep?" "This," he replied, "is the angel of punishment; and he belongs to the just angels, and is appointed to punish. He accordingly takes those who wander away from God, and who have walked in the desires and deceits of this world, and chastises them as they deserve with terrible and diverse punishments." "I would know, sir," I said, "Of what nature are these diverse tortures and punishments?" "Hear," he said, "the various tortures and punishments. The tortures are such as occur during life. For some are punished with losses, others with want, others with sicknesses of various kinds, and others with all kinds of disorder and confusion; others are insulted by unworthy persons, and exposed to suffering in many other ways: for many, becoming unstable in their plans, try many things, and none of them at all succeed, and they say they are not prosperous in their undertakings; and it does not occur to their minds that they have done evil deeds, but they blame the Lord. When, therefore, they have been afflicted with all kinds of affliction, then are they delivered unto me for good training, and they are made strong in the faith of the Lord; and for the rest of the days of their life they are subject to the Lord with pure hearts, and are successful in all their undertakings, obtaining from the Lord everything they ask; and then they glorify the Lord, that they were delivered to me, and no longer suffer any evil."

CHAPTER IV

I said to him, "Sir, explain this also to me." "What is it you ask?" he said. "Whether, sir," I continued, "they who indulge in luxury, and who are deceived, are tortured for the same period of time that they have indulged in luxury and deceit?" He said to me, "They are tortured in the same manner." ["They are tormented much less, sir," I replied;] "for those who are so luxurious and who forget God ought to be tortured seven-fold." He said to me "You are foolish, and do not understand the power of torment." "Why, sir," I said, "if I had understood it, I would not have asked you to show me." "Hear," he said, "the power of both. The time of luxury and deceit is one hour; but the hour of torment is equivalent to thirty days. If, accordingly, a man indulge in luxury for one day, and be deceived and be tortured for one day, the day of his torture is equivalent to a whole year. For all the days of luxury, therefore, there are as many years of torture to be undergone. You see, then," he continued, "that the time of luxury and deceit is very short, but that of punishment and torture long."

CHAPTER V

"Still," I said, "I do not quite understand about the time of deceit, and luxury, and torture; explain it to me more clearly." He answered, and said to me, "Your folly is persistent; and you do not wish to purify your heart, and serve God. Have a care," he added, "lest the time be fulfilled, and you be found foolish. Hear now," he added, "as you desire, that you may understand these things. He who indulges in luxury, and is deceived for one day, and who does what he wishes, is clothed with much foolishness, and does not understand the act which he does until the morrow; for he forgets what he did the day before. For luxury and deceit have no memories, on account of the folly with which they are clothed; but when punishment and torture cleave to a man for one day, he is punished and tortured for a year; for punishment and torture have powerful memories. While tortured and punished, therefore, for a whole year, he remembers at last his luxury and deceit, and knows that on their account he suffers evil. Every man, therefore, who is luxurious and deceived is thus tormented, because, although having life, they have given themselves over to death." "What kinds of luxury, sir," I asked, "are hurtful?" "Every act of a man which he performs with pleasure," he replied, "is an act of luxury; for the sharp-tempered man, when gratifying his tendency, indulges in luxury; and the adulterer, and the drunkard, and the back-biter, and the liar, and the covetous man, and the thief, and he who does things like these, gratifies his peculiar propensity, and in so doing indulges in luxury. All these acts of luxury are hurtful to the servants of God. On account of these deceits, therefore, do they suffer, who are punished and tortured. And there are also acts of luxury which save men; for many who do good indulge in luxury, being carried away by their own pleasure: this luxury, however, is beneficial to the servants of God, and gains life for such a man; but the injurious acts of luxury before enumerated bring tortures and punishment upon them; and if they continue in them and do not repent, they bring death upon themselves."

Similitude Seventh

They Who Repent Must Bring Forth Fruits Worthy of Repentance

After a few days I saw him in the same plain where I had also seen the shepherds; and he said to me, "What do you wish with me?" I said to him, "Sir, that you would order the shepherd who punishes to depart out of my house, because he afflicts me exceedingly." "It is necessary," he replied, "that you be afflicted; for thus," he continued, "did the glorious angel command concerning you, as he wishes you to be tried." "What have I done which is so bad, sir," I replied, "that I should be delivered over to this angel?" "Listen," he said: "Your sins are many, but not so great as to require that you be delivered over to this angel; but your household has committed great iniquities and sins, and the glorious angel has been incensed at them on account of their deeds; and for this reason he commanded you to be afflicted for a certain time, that they also might repent, and purify themselves from every desire of this world. When, therefore, they repent and are purified, then the angel of punishment will depart." I said to him, "Sir, if they have done such things as to incense the glorious angel against them, yet what have I done?" He replied, "They cannot be afflicted at all, unless you, the head of the house, be afflicted: for when you are afflicted, of necessity they also suffer affliction; but if you are in comfort, they can feel no affliction." "Well, sir," I said, "they have repented with their whole heart." "I know, too," he answered, "that they have repented with their whole heart: do you think, however, that the sins of those who repent are remitted? Not altogether, but he who repents must torture his own soul, and be exceedingly humble in all his conduct, and be afflicted with many kinds of affliction; and if he endure the afflictions that come upon him, He who created all things, and endued them with power, will assuredly have compassion, and will heal him; and this will He do when He sees the heart of every penitent pure from every evil thing: and it is profitable for you and for your house to suffer affliction now. But why should I say much to you? You must be afflicted, as that angel of the Lord commanded who delivered you to me. And for this give thanks to the Lord, because He has deemed you worthy of showing you beforehand this affliction, that, knowing it before it comes, you may be able to bear it with courage." I said to him, "Sir, be thou with me, and I will be able to bear all affliction." "I will be with you," he said, "and I will ask the angel of punishment to afflict you more lightly; nevertheless, you will be afflicted for a little time, and again you will be re-established in your house. Only continue humble, and serve the Lord in all purity of heart, you and your children, and your house, and walk in my commands which I enjoin upon you, and your repentance will be deep and pure; and if you observe these things with your household, every affliction will depart from you. And affliction," he added, "will depart from all who walk in these my commandments."

Similitude Eighth

The Sins of the Elect and of the Penitent are of Many Kinds, But All Will Be Rewarded According to the Measure of Their Repentance and Good Works

CHAPTER I

He showed me a large willow tree overshadowing plains and mountains, and under the shade of this willow had assembled all those who were called by the name of the Lord. And a glorious angel of the Lord, who was very tall, was standing beside the willow, having a large pruning-knife, and he was cutting little twigs from the willow and distributing them among the people that were overshadowed by the willow; and the twigs which he gave them were small, about a cubit, as it were, in length. And after they had all received the twigs, the angel laid down the pruning-knife, and that tree was sound, as I had seen it at first. And I marvelled within myself, saying, "How is the tree sound, after so many branches have been cut off?" And the Shepherd said to me, "Do not be surprised if the tree remains sound after so many branches were lopped off; [but wait,] and when you shall have seen everything, then it will be explained to you what it means." The angel who had distributed the branches among the people again asked them from them, and in the order in which they had received them were they summoned to him, and each one of them returned his branch. And the angel of the Lord took and looked at them. From some he received the branches withered and moth-eaten; those who returned branches in that state the angel of the Lord ordered to stand apart. Others, again, returned them withered, but not moth-eaten; and these he ordered to stand apart. And others returned them half-withered, and these stood apart; and others returned their branches half-withered and having cracks in them, and these stood apart. [And others returned their branches green and having cracks in them; and these stood apart.] And others returned their branches, one-half withered and the other green; and these stood apart. And others brought their branches two-thirds green and the remaining third withered; and these stood apart. And others returned them two-thirds withered and one-third green; and these stood apart. And others returned their branches nearly all green, the smallest part only, the top, being withered, but they had cracks in them; and these stood apart. And of others very little was green, but the remaining parts withered; and these stood apart. And others came bringing their branches green, as they had received them from the angel. And the majority of the crowd returned branches of that kind, and with these the angel was exceedingly pleased; and these stood apart. [And others returned their branches green and having offshoots; and these stood apart, and with these the angel was exceedingly delighted.] And others returned their branches green and with offshoots, and the offshoots had some fruit, as it were; and those men whose branches were found to be of that kind were exceedingly joyful. And the angel was exultant because of them; and the Shepherd also rejoiced greatly because of them.

CHAPTER II

And the angel of the Lord ordered crowns to be brought; and there were brought crowns, formed, as it were, of palms; and he crowned the men who had returned the branches which had offshoots and some fruit, and sent them away into the tower. And the others also he sent into the tower, those, namely, who had returned branches that were green and had offshoots but no fruit, having given them seals. And all who went into the tower had the same clothing—white as snow. And those who returned their branches green, as they had received them, he set free, giving them clothing and seals. Now after the angel had finished these things, he said to the Shepherd, "I am going away, and you will send these away within the walls, according as each one is worthy to have his dwelling. And examine their branches carefully, and so dismiss them; but examine them with care. See that no one escape you," he added; "and if any escape you, I will try them at the altar." Having said these words to the Shepherd, he departed. And after the angel had departed, the Shepherd said to me, "Let us take the branches of all these and plant them, and see if any of them will live." I said to him, "Sir, how can these withered branches live?" He answered, and said, "This tree is a willow, and of a kind that is very tenacious of life. If, therefore, the branches be planted, and receive a little moisture, many of them will live. And now let us try, and pour water upon them; and if any of them live I shall rejoice with them, and if they do not I at least will not be found neglectful." And the Shepherd bade me call them as each one was placed. And they came, rank by rank, and gave their branches to the Shepherd. And the Shepherd received the branches, and planted them in rows; and after he had planted them he poured much water upon them, so that the branches could not be seen for the water; and after the branches had drunk it in, he said to me, "Let us go, and return after a few days, and inspect all the branches; for He who created this tree wishes all those to live who received branches from it. And I also hope that the greater part of these branches which received moisture and drank of the water will live."

CHAPTER III

I said to him, "Sir, explain to me what this tree means, for I am perplexed about it, because, after so many branches have been cut off, it continues sound, and nothing appears to have been cut away from it. By this, now, I am perplexed." "Listen," he said: "This great tree that casts its shadow over plains, and mountains, and all the earth, is the law of God that was given to the whole world; and this law is the Son of God, proclaimed to the ends of the earth; and the people who are under its shadow are they who have heard the proclamation, and have believed upon Him. And the great and glorious angel Michael is he who has authority over this people, and governs them; for this is he who gave them the law into the hearts of believers: he accordingly superintends them to whom he gave it, to see if they have kept the same. And you see the branches of each one, for the branches are the law. You see, accordingly, many branches that have been rendered useless, and you will know them all—those who have not kept the law; and you will see the dwelling of each one." I said to him, "Sir, why did he dismiss some into the tower, and leave others to you?" "All," he answered, "who transgressed the law which they received from him, he left under my power for repentance; but all who have satisfied the law, and kept it, he retains under his own authority." "Who, then," I continued, "are they who were crowned, and who go to the tower?" "These are they who have suffered on account of the law; but the others, and they who returned their branches green, and with offshoots, but without fruit, are they who have been afflicted on account of the law, but who have not suffered nor denied their law; and they who returned their branches green as they had received them, are the venerable, and the just, and they who have walked carefully in a pure heart, and have kept the commandments of the Lord. And the rest you will know when I have examined those branches which have been planted and watered."

CHAPTER IV

And after a few days we came to the place, and the Shepherd sat down in the angel's place, and I stood beside him. And he said to me, "Gird yourself with pure, undressed linen made of sackcloth;" and seeing me girded, and ready to minister to him, "Summon," he said, "the men to whom belong the branches that were planted, according to the order in which each one gave them in." So I went away to the plain, and summoned them all, and they all stood in their ranks. He said to them, "Let each one pull out his own branch, and bring it to me." The first to give in were those who had them withered and cut; and because they were found to be thus withered and cut, he commanded them to stand apart. And next they gave them in who had them withered, but not cut. And some of them gave in their branches green, and some withered and eaten as by a moth. Those that gave them in green, accordingly, he ordered to stand apart; and those who gave them in dry and cut, he ordered to stand along with the first. Next they gave them in who had them half-withered and cracked; and many of them gave them in green and without cracks; and some green and with offshoots and fruits upon the offshoots, such as they had who went, after being crowned, into the tower. And some handed them in withered and eaten, and some withered and uneaten; and some as they were, half-withered and cracked. And he commanded them each one to stand apart, some towards their own rows, and others apart from them.

CHAPTER V

Then they gave in their branches who had them green, but cracked: all these gave them in green, and stood in their own row. And the Shepherd was pleased with these, because they were all changed, and had lost their cracks. And they also gave them in who had them half-green and half-withered: of some, accordingly, the branches were found completely green; of others, half-withered; of others, withered and eaten; of others, green, and having offshoots. All these were sent away, each to his own row. [Next they gave in who had them two parts green and one-third withered. Many of them gave them half-withered; and others withered and rotten; and others half-withered and cracked, and a few green. These all stood in their own row.] And they gave them in who had them green, but to a very slight extent withered and cracked. Of these, some gave them in green, and others green and with offshoots. And these also went away to their own row. Next they gave them who had a very small part green and the other parts withered. Of these the branches were found for the most part green and having offshoots, and fruit upon the offshoots, and others altogether green. With these branches the Shepherd was exceedingly pleased, because they were found in this state. And these went away, each to his own row.

CHAPTER VI

After the Shepherd had examined the branches of them all, he said to me, "I told you that this tree was tenacious of life. You see," he continued, "how many repented and were saved." "I see, sir," I replied. "That you may behold," he added, "the great mercy of the Lord, that it is great and glorious, and that He has given His Spirit to those who are worthy of repentance." "Why then, sir," I said, "did not all these repent?" He answered, "To them whose heart He saw would become pure, and obedient to Him, He gave power to repent with the whole heart. But to them whose deceit and wickedness He perceived, and saw that they intended to repent hypocritically, He did not grant repentance, lest they should again profane His name." I said to him, "Sir, show me now, with respect to those who gave in the branches, of what sort they are, and their abode, in order that they hearing it who believed, and received the seal, and broke it, and did not keep it whole, may, on coming to a knowledge of their deeds, repent, and receive from you a seal, and may glorify the Lord because He had compassion upon them, and sent you to renew their spirits." "Listen," he said: "they whose branches were found withered and moth-eaten are the apostates and traitors of the Church, who have blasphemed the Lord in their sins, and have, moreover, been ashamed of the name of the Lord by which they were called. These, therefore, at the end were lost unto God. And you see that not a single one of them repented, although they heard the words which I spake to them, which I enjoined upon you. From such life departed. And they who gave them in withered and undecayed, these also were near to them; for they were hypocrites, and introducers of strange doctrines, and subverters of the servants of God, especially of those who had sinned, not allowing them to repent, but persuading them by foolish doctrines. These, accordingly, have a hope of repentance. And you see that many of them also have repented since I spake to them, and they will still repent. But all who will not repent have lost their lives; and as many of them as repented became good, and their dwelling was appointed within the first walls; and some of them ascended even into the tower. You see, then," he said, "that repentance involves life to sinners, but non-repentance death."

CHAPTER VII

"And as many as gave in the branches half-withered and cracked, hear also about them. They whose branches were half-withered to the same extent are the wavering; for they neither live, nor are they dead. And they who have them half-withered and cracked are both waverers and slanderers, [railing against the absent,] and never at peace with one another, but always at variance. And yet to these also," he continued, "repentance is possible. You see," he said, "that some of them have repented, and there is still remaining in them," he continued, "a hope of repentance. And as many of them," he added, "as have repented, shall have their dwelling in the tower. And those of them who have been slower in repenting shall dwell within the walls. And as many as do not repent at all, but abide in their deeds, shall utterly perish. And they who gave in their branches green and cracked were always faithful and good, though emulous of each other about the foremost places, and about fame: now all these are foolish, in indulging in such a rivalry. Yet they also, being naturally good, on hearing my commandments, purified themselves, and soon repented. Their dwelling, accordingly, was in the tower. But if any one relapse into strife, he will be east out of the tower, and will lose his life. Life is the possession of all who keep the commandments of the Lord; but in the commandments there is no rivalry in regard to the first places, or glory of any kind, but in regard to patience and personal humility. Among such persons, then, is the life of the Lord, but amongst the quarrelsome and transgressors, death."

CHAPTER VIII

"And they who gave in their branches half-green and half-withered, are those who are immersed in business, and do not cleave to the saints. For this reason, the one half of them is living, and the other half dead. Many, accordingly, who heard my commands repented, and those at least who repented had their dwelling in the tower. But some of them at last fell away: these, accordingly, have not repentance, for on account of their business they blasphemed the Lord, and denied Him. They therefore lost their lives through the wickedness which they committed. And many of them doubted. These still have repentance in their power, if they repent speedily; and their abode will be in the tower. But if they are slower in repenting, they will dwell within the walls; and if they do not repent, they too have lost their lives. And they who gave in their branches two-thirds withered and one-third green, are those who have denied [the Lord] in various ways. Many, however, repented, but some of them hesitated and were in doubt. These, then, have repentance within their reach, if they repent quickly, and do not remain in their pleasures; but if they abide in their deeds, these, too, work to themselves death."

CHAPTER IX

"And they who returned their branches two-thirds withered and one-third green, are those that were faithful indeed; but after acquiring wealth, and becoming distinguished amongst the heathen, they clothed themselves with great pride, and became lofty-minded, and deserted the truth, and did not cleave to the righteous, but lived with the heathen, and this way of life became more agreeable to them. They did not, however, depart from God, but remained in the faith, although not working the works of faith. Many of them accordingly repented, and their dwelling was in the tower. And others continuing to live until the end with the heathen, and being corrupted by their vain glories, [departed from God, serving the works and deeds of the heathen.] These were reckoned with the heathen. But others of them hesitated, not hoping to be saved on account of the deeds which they had done; while others were in doubt, and caused divisions among themselves. To those, therefore, who were in doubt on account of their deeds, repentance is still open; but their repentance ought to be speedy, that their dwelling may be in the tower. And to those who do not repent, but abide in their pleasures, death is near."

CHAPTER X

"And they who give in their branches green, but having the tips withered and cracked, these were always good, and faithful, and distinguished before God; but they sinned a very little through indulging small desires, and finding little faults with one another. But on hearing my words the greater part of them quickly repented, and their dwelling was upon the tower. Yet some of them were in doubt; and certain of them who were in doubt wrought greater dissension. Among these, therefore, is hope of repentance, because they were always good; and with difficulty will any one of them perish. And they who gave up their branches withered, but having a very small part green, are those who believed only, yet continue working the works of iniquity. They never, however, departed from God, but gladly bore His name, and joyfully received His servants into their houses. Having accordingly heard of this repentance, they unhesitatingly repented, and practice all virtue and righteousness; and some of them even [suffered, being willingly put to death], knowing their deeds which they had done. Of all these, therefore, the dwelling shall be in the tower."

CHAPTER XI

And after he had finished the explanations of all the branches, he said to me, "Go and tell them to every one, that they may repent, and they shall live unto God. Because the Lord, having had compassion on all men, has sent me to give repentance, although some are not worthy of it on account of their works; but the Lord, being long-suffering, desires those who were called by His Son to be saved." I said to him, "Sir, I hope that all who have heard them will repent; for I am persuaded that each one, on coming to a knowledge of his own works, and fearing the Lord, will repent." He answered me, and said, "All who with their whole heart shall purify themselves from their wickedness before enumerated, and shall add no more to their sins, will receive healing from the Lord for their former transgressions, if they do not hesitate at these commandments; and they will live unto God. But do you walk in my commandments, and live." Having shown me these things, and spoken all these words, he said to me, "And the rest I will show you after a few days."

Similitude Ninth

The Great Mysteries in the Building of the Militant and Triumphant Church

CHAPTER I

After I had written down the commandments and similitudes of the Shepherd, the angel of repentance, he came to me and said, "I wish to explain to you what the Holy Spirit that spake with you in the form of the Church showed you, for that Spirit is the Son of God. For, as you were somewhat weak in the flesh, it was not explained to you by the angel. When, however, you were strengthened by the Spirit, and your strength was increased, so that you were able to see the angel also, then accordingly was the building of the tower shown you by the Church. In a noble and solemn manner did you see everything as if shown you by a virgin; but now you see [them] through the same Spirit as if shown by an angel. You must, however, learn everything from me with greater accuracy. For I was sent for this purpose by the glorious angel to dwell in your house, that you might see all things with power, entertaining no fear, even as it was before." And he led me away into Arcadia, to a round hill; and he placed me on the top of the hill, and showed me a large plain, and round about the plain twelve mountains, all having different forms. The first was black as soot; and the second bare, without grass; and the third full of thorns and thistles; and the fourth with grass half-withered, the upper parts of the plants green, and the parts about the roots withered; and some of the grasses, when the sun scorched them, became withered. And the fifth mountain had green grass, and was ragged. And the sixth mountain was quite full of clefts, some small and others large; and the clefts were grassy, but the plants were not very vigorous, but rather, as it were, decayed. The seventh mountain, again, had cheerful pastures, and the whole mountain was blooming, and every kind of cattle and birds were feeding upon that mountain; and the more the cattle and the birds ate, the more the grass of that mountain flourished. And the eighth mountain was full of fountains, and every kind of the Lord's creatures drank of the fountains of that mountain. But the ninth mountain [had no water at all, and was wholly a desert, and had within it deadly serpents, which destroy men. And the tenth mountain] had very large trees, and was completely shaded, and under the shadow of the trees sheep lay resting and ruminating. And the eleventh mountain was very thickly wooded, and those trees were productive, being adorned with various sorts of fruits, so that any one seeing them would desire to eat of their fruits. The twelfth mountain, again, was wholly white, and its aspect was cheerful, and the mountain in itself was very beautiful.

CHAPTER II

And in the middle of the plain he showed me a large white rock that had arisen out of the plain. And the rock was more lofty than the mountains, rectangular in shape, so as to be capable of containing the whole world: and that rock was old, having a gate cut out of it; and the cutting out of the gate seemed to me as if recently done. And the gate glittered to such a degree under the sunbeams, that I marvelled at the splendour of the gate; and round about the gate were standing twelve virgins. The four who stood at the corners seemed to me more distinguished than the others—they were all, however, distinguished—and they were standing at the four parts of the gate; two virgins between each part. And they were clothed with linen tunics, and gracefully girded, having their right shoulders exposed, as if about to bear some burden. Thus they stood ready; for they were exceedingly cheerful and eager. After I had seen these things, I marvelled in myself, because I was beholding great and glorious sights. And again I was perplexed about the virgins, because, although so delicate, they were standing courageously, as if about to carry the whole heavens. And the Shepherd said to me "Why are you reasoning in yourself, and perplexing your mind, and distressing yourself? for the things which you cannot understand, do not attempt to comprehend, as if you were wise; but ask the Lord, that you may receive understanding and know them. You cannot see what is behind you, but you see what is before. Whatever, then, you cannot see, let alone, and do not torment yourself about it: but what you see, make yourself master of it, and do not waste your labour about other things; and I will explain to you everything that I show you. Look therefore, on the things that remain."

CHAPTER III

I saw six men come, tall, and distinguished, and similar in appearance, and they summoned a multitude of men. And they who came were also tall men, and handsome, and powerful; and the six men commanded them to build a tower above the rock. And great was the noise of those men who came to build the tower, as they ran hither and thither around the gate. And the virgins who stood around the gate told the men to hasten to build the tower. Now the virgins had spread out their hands, as if about to receive something from the men. And the six men commanded stones to ascend out of a certain pit, and to go to the building of the tower. And there went up ten shining rectangular stones, not hewn in a quarry. And the six men called the virgins, and bade them carry all the stones that were intended for the building, and to pass through the gate, and give them to the men who were about to build the tower. And the virgins put upon one another the ten first stones which had ascended from the pit, and carried them together, each stone by itself.

CHAPTER IV

And as they stood together around the gate, those who seemed to be strong carried them, and they stooped down under the corners of the stone; and the others stooped down under the sides of the stones. And in this way they carried all the stones. And they carried them through the gate as they were commanded, and gave them to the men for the tower; and they took the stones and proceeded with the building. Now the tower was built upon the great rock, and above the gate. Those ten stones were prepared as the foundation for the building of the tower. And the rock and gate were the support of the whole of the tower. And after the ten stones other twenty [five] came up out of the pit, and these were fitted into the building of the tower, being carried by the virgins as before. And after these ascended thirty-five. And these in like manner were fitted into the tower. And after these other forty stones came up; and all these were cast into the building of the tower, [and there were four rows in the foundation of the tower,] and they ceased ascending from the pit. And the builders also ceased for a little. And again the six men commanded the multitude of the crowd to bear stones from the mountains for the building of the tower. They were accordingly brought from all the mountains of various colours, and being hewn by the men were given to the virgins; and the virgins carried them through the gate, and gave them for the building of the tower. And when the stones of various colours were placed in the building, they all became white alike, and lost their different colours. And certain stones were given by the men for the building, and these did not become shining; but as they were placed, such also were they found to remain: for they were not given by the virgins, nor carried through the gate. These stones, therefore, were not in keeping with the others in the building of the tower. And the six men, seeing these unsuitable stones in the building, commanded them to be taken away, and to be carried away down to their own place whence they had been taken; [and being removed one by one, they were laid aside; and] they say to the men who brought the stones, "Do not ye bring any stones at all for the building, but lay them down beside the tower, that the virgins may carry them through the gate, and may give them for the building. For unless," they said, "they be carried through the gate by the hands of the virgins, they cannot change their colours: do not toil, therefore," they said, "to no purpose."

CHAPTER V

And on that day the building was finished, but the tower was not completed; for additional building was again about to be added, and there was a cessation in the building. And the six men commanded the builders all to withdraw a little distance, and to rest, but enjoined the virgins not to withdraw from the tower; and it seemed to me that the virgins had been left to guard the tower. Now after all had withdrawn, and were resting themselves, I said to the Shepherd, "What is the reason that the building of the tower was not finished?" "The tower," he answered, "cannot be finished just yet, until the Lord of it come and examine the building, in order that, if any of the stones be found to be decayed, he may change them: for the tower is built according to his pleasure." "I would like to know, sir," I said, "what is the meaning of the building of this tower, and what the rock and gate, and the mountains, and the virgins mean, and the stones that ascended from the pit, and were not hewn, but came as they were to the building. Why, in the first place, were ten stones placed in the foundation, then twenty-five, then thirty-five, then forty? and I wish also to know about the stones that went to the building, and were again taken out and returned to their own place? On all these points put my mind at rest, sir, and explain them to me." "If you are not found to be curious about trifles," he replied, "you shall know everything. For after a few days [we shall come hither, and you will see the other things that happen to this tower, and will know accurately all the similitudes." After a few days] we came to the place where we sat down. And he said to me, "Let us go to the tower; for the master of the tower is coming to examine it." And we came to the tower, and there was no one at all near it, save the virgins only. And the Shepherd asked the virgins if perchance the master of the tower had come; and they replied that he was about to come to examine the building.

CHAPTER VI

And, behold, after a little I see an array of many men coming, and in the midst of them one man of so remarkable a size as to overtop the tower. And the six men who had worked upon the building were with him, and many other honourable men were around him. And the virgins who kept the tower ran forward and kissed him, and began to walk near him around the tower. And that man examined the building carefully, feeling every stone separately; and holding a rod in his hand, he struck every stone in the building three times. And when he struck them, some of them became black as soot, and some appeared as if covered with scabs, and some cracked, and some mutilated, and some neither white nor black, and some rough and not in keeping with the other stones, and some having [very many] stains: such were the varieties of decayed stones that were found in the building. He ordered all these to be taken out of the tower, and to be laid down beside it, and other stones to be brought and put in their stead. [And the builders asked him from what mountain he wished them to be brought and put in their place.] And he did not command them to be brought from the mountains, [but he bade them be brought from a certain plain which was near at hand.] And the plain was dug up, and shining rectangular stones were found, and some also of a round shape; and all the stones which were in that plain were brought, and carried through the gate by the virgins. And the rectangular stones were hewn, and put in place of those that were taken away; but the rounded stones were not put into the building, because they were hard to hew, and appeared to yield slowly to the chisel; they were deposited, however, beside the tower, as if intended to be hewn and used in the building, for they were exceedingly brilliant.

CHAPTER VII

The glorious man, the lord of the whole tower, having accordingly finished these alterations, called to him the Shepherd, and delivered to him all the stones that were lying beside the tower, that had been rejected from the building, and said to him, "Carefully clean all these stones, and put aside such for the building of the tower as may harmonize with the others; and those that do not, throw far away from the tower." [Having given these orders to the Shepherd, he departed from the tower], with all those with whom he had come. Now the virgins were standing around the tower, keeping it. I said again to the Shepherd, "Can these stones return to the building of the tower, after being rejected?" He answered me, and said, "Do you see these stones?" "I see them, sir," I replied. "The greater part of these stones," he said, "I will hew, and put into the building, and they will harmonize with the others." "How, sir," I said, "can they, after being cut all round about, fill up the same space?" He answered, "Those that shall be found small will be thrown into the middle of the building, and those that are larger will be placed on the outside, and they will hold them together." Having spoken these words, he said to me, "Let us go, and after two days let us come and clean these stones, and cast them into the building; for all things around the tower must be cleaned, lest the Master come suddenly and find the places about the tower dirty, and be displeased, and these stones be not returned for the building of the tower, and I also shall seem to be neglectful towards the Master." And after two days we came to the tower, and he said to me, "Let us examine all the stones, and ascertain those which may return to the building." I said to him, "Sir, let us examine them!"

CHAPTER VIII

And beginning, we first examined the black stones. And such as they had been taken out of the building, were they found to remain; and the Shepherd ordered them to be removed out of the tower, and to be placed apart. Next he examined those that had scabs; and he took and hewed many of these, and commanded the virgins to take them up and cast them into the building. And the virgins lifted them up, and put them in the middle of the building of the tower. And the rest he ordered to be laid down beside the black ones; for these, too, were found to be black. He next examined those that had cracks; and he hewed many of these, and commanded them to be carried by the virgins to the building: and they were placed on the outside, because they were found to be sounder than the others; but the rest, on account of the multitude of the cracks, could not be hewn, and for this reason, therefore, they were rejected from the building of the tower. He next examined the chipped stones, and many amongst these were found to be black, and some to have great cracks. And these also he commanded to be laid down along with those which had been rejected. But the remainder, after being cleaned and hewn, he commanded to be placed in the building. And the virgins took them up, and fitted them into the middle of the building of the tower, for they were somewhat weak. He next examined those that were half white and half black, and many of them were found to be black. And he commanded these also to be taken away along with those which had been rejected. And the rest were all taken away by the virgins; for, being white, they were fitted by the virgins themselves into the building. And they were placed upon the outside, because they were found to be sound, so as to be able to support those which were placed in the middle, for no part of them at all was chipped. He next examined those that were rough and hard; and a few of them were rejected because they could not be hewn, as they were found exceedingly hard. But the rest of them were hewn, and carried by the virgins, and fitted into the middle of the building of the tower; for they were somewhat weak. He next examined those that had stains; and of these a very few were black, and were thrown aside with the others; but the greater part were found to be bright, and these were fitted by the virgins into the building, but on account of their strength were placed on the outside.

CHAPTER IX

He next came to examine the white and rounded stones, and said to me, "What are we to do with these stones?" "How do I know, sir?" I replied. "Have you no intentions regarding them?" "Sir," I answered, "I am not acquainted with this art, neither am I a stone-cutter, nor can I tell." "Do you not see," he said, "that they are exceedingly round? and if I wish to make them rectangular, a large portion of them must be cut away; for some of them must of necessity be put into the building." "If therefore," I said, "they must, why do you torment yourself, and not at once choose for the building those which you prefer, and fit them into it?" He selected the larger ones among them, and the shining ones, and hewed them; and the virgins carried and fitted them into the outside parts of the building. And the rest which remained over were carried away, and laid down on the plain from which they were brought. They were not, however, rejected, "because," he said, "there remains yet a little addition to be built to the tower. And the lord of this tower wishes all the stones to be fitted into the building, because they are exceedingly bright." And twelve women were called, very beautiful in form, clothed in black, and with dishevelled hair. And these women seemed to me to be fierce. But the Shepherd commanded them to lift the stones that were rejected from the building, and to carry them away to the mountains from which they had been brought. And they were merry, and carried away all the stones, and put them in the place whence they had been taken. Now after all the stones were removed, and there was no longer a single one lying around the tower, he said, "Let us go round the tower and see, lest there be any defect in it." So I went round the tower along with him. And the Shepherd, seeing that the tower was beautifully built, rejoiced exceedingly; for the tower was built in such a way, that, on seeing it, I coveted the building of it, for it was constructed as if built of one stone, without a single joining. And the stone seemed as if hewn out of the rock; having to me the appearance of a monolith.

CHAPTER X

And as I walked along with him, I was full of joy, beholding so many excellent things. And the Shepherd said to me, "Go and bring unslacked lime and fine-baked clay, that I may fill up the forms of the stones that were taken and thrown into the building; for everything about the tower must be smooth." And I did as he commanded me, and brought it to him. "Assist me," he said, "and the work will soon be finished." He accordingly filled up the forms of the stones that were returned to the building, and commanded the places around the tower to be swept and to be cleaned; and the virgins took brooms and swept the place, and carried all the dirt out of the tower, and brought water, and the ground around the tower became cheerful and very beautiful. Says the Shepherd to me, "Everything has been cleared away; if the lord of the tower come to inspect it, he can have no fault to find with us." Having spoken these words, he wished to depart; but I laid hold of him by the wallet, and began to adjure him by the Lord that he would explain what he had showed me. He said to me, "I must rest a little, and then I shall explain to you everything; wait for me here until I return." I said to him, "Sir, what can I do here alone?" "You are not alone," he said, "for these virgins are with you." "Give me in charge to them, then," I replied. The Shepherd called them to him, and said to them, "I entrust him to you until I come," and went away. And I was alone with the virgins; and they were rather merry, but were friendly to me, especially the four more distinguished of them.

CHAPTER XI

The virgins said to me, "The Shepherd does not come here to-day." "What, then," said I, "am I to do?" They replied, "Wait for him until he comes; and if he comes he will converse with you, and if he does not come you will remain here with us until he does come." I said to them, "I will wait for him until it is late; and if he does not arrive, I will go away into the house, and come back early in the morning." And they answered and said to me, "You were entrusted to us; you cannot go away from us." "Where, then," I said, "am I to remain?" "You will sleep with us," they replied, "as a brother, and not as a husband: for you are our brother, and for the time to come we intend to abide with you, for we love you exceedingly!" But I was ashamed to remain with them. And she who seemed to be the first among them began to kiss me. [And the others seeing her kissing me, began also to kiss me], and to lead me round the tower, and to play with me. And I, too, became like a young man, and began to play with them: for some of them formed a chorus, and others danced, and others sang; and I, keeping silence, walked with them around the tower, and was merry with them. And when it grew late I wished to go into the house; and they would not let me, but detained me. So I remained with them during the night, and slept beside the tower. Now the virgins spread their linen tunics on the ground, and made me lie down in the midst of them; and they did nothing at all but pray; and I without ceasing prayed with them, and not less than they. And the virgins rejoiced because I thus prayed. And I remained there with the virgins until the next day at the second hour. Then the Shepherd returned, and said to the virgins, "Did you offer him any insult?" "Ask him," they said. I said to him, "Sir, I was delighted that I remained with them." "On what," he asked, "did you sup?" "I supped, sir," I replied, "on the words of the Lord the whole night." "Did they receive you well?" he inquired. "Yes, sir," I answered. "Now," he said, "what do you wish to hear first?" "I wish to hear in the order," I said, "in which you showed me from the beginning. I beg of you, sir, that as I shall ask you, so also you will give me the explanation." "As you wish," he replied, "so also will I explain to you, and will conceal nothing at all from you."

CHAPTER XII

"First of all, sir," I said, "explain this to me: What is the meaning of the rock and the gate?" "This rock," he answered, "and this gate are the Son of God." "How, sir?" I said; "the rock is old, and the gate is new." "Listen," he said, "and understand, O ignorant man. The Son of God is older than all His creatures, so that He was a fellow-councillor with the Father in His work of creation: for this reason is He old." "And why is the gate new, sir?" I said. "Because," he answered, "He became manifest in the last days of the dispensation: for this reason the gate was made new, that they who are to be saved by it might enter into the kingdom of God. You saw," he said, "that those stones which came in through the gate were used for the building of the tower, and that those which did not come, were again thrown back to their own place?" "I saw, sir," I replied. "In like manner," he continued, "no one shall enter into the kingdom of God unless he receive His holy name. For if you desire to enter into a city, and that city is surrounded by a wall, and has but one gate, can you enter into that city save through the gate which it has?" "Why, how can it be otherwise, sir?" I said. "If, then, you cannot enter into the city except through its gate, so, in like manner, a man cannot otherwise enter into the kingdom of God than by the name of His beloved Son. You saw," he added, "the multitude who were building the tower?" "I saw them, sir," I said. "Those," he said, "are all glorious angels, and by them accordingly is the Lord surrounded. And the gate is the Son of God. This is the one entrance to the Lord. In no other way, then, shall any one enter in to Him except through His Son. You saw," he continued, "the six men, and the tall and glorious man in the midst of them, who walked round the tower, and rejected the stones from the building?" "I saw him, sir," I answered. "The glorious man," he said, "is the Son of God, and those six glorious angels are those who support Him on the right hand and on the left. None of these glorious angels," he continued, "will enter in unto God apart from Him. Whosoever does not receive His name, shall not enter into the kingdom of God."

CHAPTER XIII

"And the tower," I asked, "what does it mean?" "This tower," he replied, "is the Church." "And these virgins, who are they?" "They are holy spirits, and men cannot otherwise be found in the kingdom of God unless these have put their clothing upon them: for if you receive the name only, and do not receive from them the clothing, they are of no advantage to you. For these virgins are the powers of the Son of God. If you bear His name but possess not His power, it will be in vain that you bear His name. Those stones," he continued, "which you saw rejected bore His name, but did not put on the clothing of the virgins." "Of what nature is their clothing, sir?" I asked. "Their very names," he said, "are their clothing. Every one who bears the name of the Son of God, ought to bear the names also of these; for the Son Himself bears the names of these virgins. As many stones," he continued, "as you saw [come into the building of the tower through the hands] of these virgins, and remaining, have been clothed with their strength. For this reason you see that the tower became of one stone with the rock. So also they who have believed on the Lord through His Son, and are clothed with these spirits, shall become one spirit, one body, and the colour of their garments shall be one. And the dwelling of such as bear the names of the virgins is in the tower." "Those stones, sir, that were rejected," I inquired, "on what account were they rejected? for they passed through the gate, and were placed by the hands of the virgins in the building of the tower." "Since you take an interest in everything," he replied, "and examine minutely, hear about the stones that were rejected. These all," he said, "received the name of God, and they received also the strength of these virgins. Having received, then, these spirits, they were made strong, and were with the servants of God; and theirs was one spirit, and one body, and one clothing. For they were of the same mind, and wrought righteousness. After a certain time, however, they were persuaded by the women whom you saw clothed in black, and having their shoulders exposed and their hair dishevelled, and beautiful in appearance. Having seen these women, they desired to have them, and clothed themselves with their strength, and put off the strength of the virgins. These, accordingly, were rejected from the house of God, and were given over to these women. But they who were not deceived by the beauty of these women remained in the house of God. You have," he said, "the explanation of those who were rejected."

CHAPTER XIV

"What, then, sir," I said, "if these men, being such as they are, repent and put away their desires after these women, and return again to the virgins, and walk in their strength and in their works, shall they not enter into the house of God?" "They shall enter in," he said, "if they put away the works of these women, and put on again the strength of the virgins, and walk in their works. For on this account was there a cessation in the building, in order that, if these repent, they may depart into the building of the tower. But if they do not repent, then others will come in their place, and these at the end will be cast out. For all these things I gave thanks to the Lord, because He had pity on all that call upon His name; and sent the angel of repentance to us who sinned against Him, and renewed our spirit; and when we were already destroyed, and had no hope of life, He restored us to newness of life." "Now, sir," I continued, "show me why the tower was not built upon the ground, but upon the rock and upon the gate." "Are you still," he said, "without sense and understanding?" "I must, sir," I said, "ask you of all things, because I am wholly unable to understand them; for all these things are great and glorious, and difficult for man to understand." "Listen," he said: "the name of the Son of God is great, and cannot be contained, and supports the whole world. If, then, the whole creation is supported by the Son of God, what think ye of those who are called by Him, and bear the name of the Son of God, and walk in His commandments? do you see what kind of persons He supports? Those who bear His name with their whole heart. He Himself, accordingly, became a foundation to them, and supports them with joy, because they are not ashamed to bear His name."

CHAPTER XV.

"Explain to me, sir," I said, "the names of these virgins, and of those women who were clothed in black raiment." "Hear," he said, "the names of the stronger virgins who stood at the corners. The first is Faith, the second Continence, the third Power, the fourth Patience. And the others standing in the midst of these have the following names: Simplicity, Innocence, Purity, Cheerfulness, Truth, Understanding, Harmony, Love. He who bears these names and that of the Son of God will be able to enter into the kingdom of God. Hear, also," he continued, "the names of the women who had the black garments; and of these four are stronger than the rest. The first is Unbelief, the second: Incontinence, the third Disobedience, the fourth Deceit. And their followers are called Sorrow, Wickedness, Wantonness, Anger, Falsehood, Folly, Backbiting, Hatred. The servant of God who bears these names shall see, indeed, the kingdom of God, but shall not enter into it." "And the stones, sir," I said, "which were taken out of the pit and fitted into the building: what are they?" "The first," he said, "the ten, viz., that were placed as a foundation, are the first generation, and the twenty-five the second generation, of righteous men; and the thirty-five are the prophets of God and His ministers; and the forty are the apostles and teachers of the preaching of the Son of God." "Why, then, sir," I asked, "did the virgins carry these stones also through the gate, and give them for the building of the tower?" "Because," he answered, "these were the first who bore these spirits, and they never departed from each other, neither the spirits from the men nor the men from the spirits, but the spirits remained with them until their falling asleep. And unless they had had these spirits with them, they would not have been of use for the building of this tower."

CHAPTER XVI

"Explain to me a little further, sir," I said. "What is it that you desire?" he asked. "Why, sir," I said, "did these stones ascend out of the pit, and be applied to the building of the tower, after having borne these spirits?" "They were obliged," he answered, "to ascend through water in order that they might be made alive; for, unless they laid aside the deadness of their life, they could not in any other way enter into the kingdom of God. Accordingly, those also who fell asleep received the seal of the Son of God. For," he continued, "before a man bears the name of the Son of God he is dead; but when he receives the seal he lays aside his deadness, and obtains life. The seal, then, is the water: they descend into the water dead, and they arise alive. And to them, accordingly, was this seal preached, and they made use of it that they might enter into the kingdom of God." "Why, sir," I asked, "did the forty stones also ascend with them out of the pit, having already received the seal?" "Because," he said, "these apostles and teachers who preached the name of the Son of God, after falling asleep in the power and faith of the Son of God, preached it not only to those who were asleep, but themselves also gave them the seal of the preaching. Accordingly they descended with them into the water, and again ascended. [But these descended alive and rose up again alive; whereas they who had previously fallen asleep descended dead, but rose up again alive.] By these, then, were they quickened and made to know the name of the Son of God. For this reason also did they ascend with them, and were fitted along with them into the building of the tower, and, untouched by the chisel, were built in along with them. For they slept in righteousness and in great purity, but only they had not this seal. You have accordingly the explanation of these also."

CHAPTER XVII

"I understand, sir," I replied. "Now, sir," I continued, "explain to me, with respect to the mountains, why their forms are various and diverse." "Listen," he said: "these mountains are the twelve tribes, which inhabit the whole world. The Son of God, accordingly, was preached unto them by the apostles." "But why are the mountains of various kinds, some having one form, and others another? Explain that to me, sir." "Listen," he answered: "these twelve tribes that inhabit the whole world are twelve nations. And they vary in prudence and understanding. As numerous, then, as are the varieties of the mountains which you saw, are also the diversities of mind and understanding among these nations. And I will explain to you the actions of each one." "First, sir," I said, "explain this: why, when the mountains are so diverse, their stones, when placed in the building, became one colour, shining like those also that had ascended out of the pit." "Because," he said, "all the nations that dwell under heaven were called by hearing and believing upon the name of the Son of God. Having, therefore, received the seal, they had one understanding and one mind; and their faith became one, and their love one, and with the name they bore also the spirits of the virgins. On this account the building of the tower became of one colour, bright as the sun. But after they had entered into the same place, and became one body, certain of these defiled themselves, and were expelled from the race of the righteous, and became again what they were before, or rather worse."

CHAPTER XVIII

"How, sir," I said, "did they become worse, after having known God?" "He that does not know God," he answered, "and practices evil, receives a certain chastisement for his wickedness; but he that has known God, ought not any longer to do evil, but to do good. If, accordingly, when he ought to do good, he do evil, does not he appear to do greater evil than he who does not know God? For this reason, they who have not known God and do evil are condemned to death; but they who have known God, and have seen His mighty works, and still continue in evil, shall be chastised doubly, and shall die for ever. In this way, then, will the Church of God be purified. For as you saw the stones rejected from the tower, and delivered to the evil spirits, and cast out thence, so [they also shall be cast out, and] there shall be one body of the purified; as the tower also became, as it were, of one stone after its purification. In like manner also shall it be with the Church of God, after it has been purified, and has rejected the wicked, and the hypocrites, and the blasphemers, and the waverers, and those who commit wickedness of different kinds. After these have been cast away, the Church of God shall be one body, of one mind, of one understanding, of one faith, of one love. And then the Son of God will be exceeding glad, and shall rejoice over them, because He has received His people pure." "All these things, sir," I said, "are great and glorious."

"Moreover, sir," I said, "explain to me the power and the actions of each one of the mountains, that every soul, trusting in the Lord, and hearing it, may glorify His great, and marvellous, and glorious name." "Hear," he said, "the diversity of the mountains and of the twelve nations."

CHAPTER XIX

"From the first mountain, which was black, they that believed are the following: apostates and blasphemers against the Lord, and betrayers of the servants of God. To these repentance is not open; but death lies before them, and on this account also are they black, for their race is a lawless one. And from the second mountain, which was bare, they who believed are the following: hypocrites, and teachers of wickedness. And these, accordingly, are like the former, not having any fruits of righteousness; for as their mountain was destitute of fruit, so also such men have a name indeed, but are empty of faith, and there is no fruit of truth in them. They indeed have repentance in their power, if they repent quickly; but if they are slow in so doing, they shall die along with the former." "Why, sir," I said, "have these repentance, but the former not? for their actions are nearly the same." "On this account," he said, "have these repentance, because they did not blaspheme their Lord, nor become betrayers of the servants of God; but on account of their desire of possessions they became hypocritical, and each one taught according to the desires of men that were sinners. But they will suffer a certain punishment; and repentance is before them, because they were not blasphemers or traitors."

CHAPTER XX

"And from the third mountain, which had thorns and thistles, they who believed are the following. There are some of them rich, and others immersed in much business. The thistles are the rich, and the thorns are they who are immersed in much business. Those, [accordingly, who are entangled in many various kinds of business, do not] cleave to the servants of God, but wander away, being choked by their business transactions; and the rich cleave with difficulty to the servants of God, fearing lest these should ask something of them. Such persons, accordingly, shall have difficulty in entering the kingdom of God. For as it is disagreeable to walk among thistles with naked feet, so also it is hard for such to enter the kingdom of God. But to all these repentance, and that speedy, is open, in order that what they did not do in former times they may make up for in these days, and do some good, and they shall live unto God. But if they abide in their deeds, they shall be delivered to those women, who will put them to death."

CHAPTER XXI

"And from the fourth mountain, which had much grass, the upper parts of the plants green, and the parts about the roots withered, and some also scorched by the sun, they who believed are the following: the doubtful, and they who have the Lord upon their lips, but have Him not in their heart. On this account their foundations are withered, and have no strength; and their words alone live, while their works are dead. Such persons are [neither alive nor] dead. They resemble, therefore, the waverers: for the wavering are neither withered nor green, being neither living nor dead. For as their blades, on seeing the sun, were withered, so also the wavering, when they hear of affliction, on account of their fear, worship idols, and are ashamed of the name of their Lord. Such, then, are neither alive nor dead. But these also may yet live, if they repent quickly; and if they do not repent, they are already delivered to the women, who take away their life."

CHAPTER XXII

"And from the fifth mountain, which had green grass, and was rugged, they who believed are the following: believers, indeed, but slow to learn, and obstinate, and pleasing themselves, wishing to know everything, and knowing nothing at all. On account of this obstinacy of theirs, understanding departed from them, and foolish senselessness entered into them. And they praise themselves as having wisdom, and desire to become teachers, although destitute of sense. On account, therefore, of this loftiness of mind, many became vain, exalting themselves: for self-will and empty confidence is a great demon. Of these, accordingly, many were rejected, but some repented and believed, and subjected themselves to those that had understanding, knowing their own foolishness. And to the rest of this class repentance is open; for they were not wicked, but rather foolish, and without understanding. If these therefore repent, they will live unto God; but if they do not repent, they shall have their dwelling with the women who wrought wickedness among them."

CHAPTER XXIII

"And those from the sixth mountain, which had clefts large and small, and decayed grass in the clefts, who believed, were the following: they who occupy the small clefts are those who bring charges against one another, and by reason of their slanders have decayed in the faith. Many of them, however, repented; and the rest also will repent when they hear my commandments, for their slanders are small, and they will quickly repent. But they who occupy the large clefts are persistent in their slanders, and vindictive in their anger against each other. These, therefore, were thrown away from the tower, and rejected from having a part in its building. Such persons, accordingly, shall have difficulty in living. If our God and Lord, who rules over all things, and has power over all His creation, does not remember evil against those who confess their sins, but is merciful, does man, who is corruptible and full of sins, remember evil against a fellow-man, as if he were able to destroy or to save him? I, the angel of repentance, say unto you, As many of you as are of this way of thinking, lay it aside, and repent, and the Lord will heal your former sins, if you purify yourselves from this demon; but if not, you will be delivered over to him for death."

CHAPTER XXIV

"And those who believed from the seventh mountain, on which the grass was green and flourishing, and the whole of the mountain fertile, and every kind of cattle and the fowls of heaven were feeding on the grass on this mountain, and the grass on which they pastured became more abundant, were the following: they were always simple, and harmless, and blessed, bringing no charges against one another, but always rejoicing greatly because of the servants of God, and being clothed with the holy spirit of these virgins, and always having pity on every man, and giving aid from their own labour to every man, without reproach and without hesitation. The Lord, therefore, seeing their simplicity and all their meekness, multiplied them amid the labours of their hands, and gave them grace in all their doings. And I, the angel of repentance, say to you who are such, Continue to be such as these, and your seed will never be blotted out; for the Lord has made trial of you, and inscribed you in the number of us, and the whole of your seed will dwell with the Son of God; for ye have received of His Spirit."

CHAPTER XXV

"And they who believed from the eighth mountain, where were the many fountains, and where all the creatures of God drank of the fountains, were the following: apostles, and teachers, who preached to the whole world, and who taught solemnly and purely the word of the Lord, and did not at all fall into evil desires, but walked always in righteousness and truth, according as they had received the Holy Spirit. Such persons, therefore, shall enter in with the angels."

CHAPTER XXVI

"And they who believed from the ninth mountain, which was deserted, and had in it creeping things and wild beasts which destroy men, were the following: they who had the stains as servants, who discharged their duty ill, and who plundered widows and orphans of their livelihood, and gained possessions for themselves from the ministry, which they had received. If, therefore, they remain under the dominion of the same desire, they are dead, and there is no hope of life for them; but if they repent, and finish their ministry in a holy manner, they shall be able to live. And they who were covered with scabs are those who have denied their Lord, and have not returned to Him again; but becoming withered and desert-like, and not cleaving to the servants of God, but living in solitude, they destroy their own souls. For as a vine, when left within an enclosure, and meeting with neglect, is destroyed, and is made desolate by the weeds, and in time grows wild, and is no longer of any use to its master, so also are such men as have given themselves up, and become useless to their Lord, from having contracted savage habits. These men, therefore, have repentance in their power, unless they are found to have denied from the heart; but if any one is found to have denied from the heart, I do not know if he may live. And I say this not for these present days, in order that any one who has denied may obtain repentance, for it is impossible for him to be saved who now intends to deny his Lord; but to those who denied Him long ago, repentance seems to be possible. If, therefore, any one intends to repent, let him do so quickly, before the tower is completed; for if not, he will be utterly destroyed by the women. And the chipped stones are the deceitful and the slanderers; and the wild beasts which you saw on the ninth mountain, are the same. For as wild beasts destroy and kill a man by their poison, so also do the words of such men destroy and ruin a man. These, accordingly, are mutilated in their faith, on account of the deeds which they have done in themselves; yet some repented, and were saved. And the rest, who are of such a character, can be saved if they repent; but if they do not repent, they will perish with those women, whose strength they have assumed."

CHAPTER XXVII

"And from the tenth mountain, where were trees which overshadowed certain sheep, they who believed were the following: bishops given to hospitality, who always gladly received into their houses the servants of God, without dissimulation. And the bishops never failed to protect, by their service, the widows, and those who were in want, and always maintained a holy conversation. All these, accordingly, shall be protected by the Lord for ever. They who do these things are honourable before God, and their place is already with the angels, if they remain to the end serving God."

CHAPTER XXVIII

"And from the eleventh mountain, where were trees full of fruits, adorned with fruits of various kinds, they who believed were the following: they who suffered for the name of the Son of God, and who also suffered cheerfully with their whole heart, and laid down their lives." "Why, then, sir," I said, "do all these trees bear fruit, and some of them fairer than the rest?" "Listen," he said:

"all who once suffered for the name of the Lord are honourable before God; and of all these the sins were remitted, because they suffered for the name of the Son of God. And why their fruits are of various kinds, and some of them superior, listen. All," he continued, "who were brought before the authorities and were examined, and did not deny, but suffered cheerfully—these are held in greater honour with God, and of these the fruit is superior; but all who were cowards, and in doubt, and who reasoned in their hearts whether they would deny or confess, and yet suffered, of these the fruit is less, because that suggestion came into their hearts; for that suggestion—that a servant should deny his Lord—is evil. Have a care, therefore, ye who are planning such things, lest that suggestion remain in your hearts, and ye perish unto God. And ye who suffer for His name ought to glorify God, because He deemed you worthy to bear His name, that all your sins might be healed. [Therefore, rather deem yourselves happy], and think that ye have done a great thing, if any of you suffer on account of God. The Lord bestows upon you life, and ye do not understand, for your sins were heavy; but if you had not suffered for the name of the Lord, ye would have died to God on account of your sins. These things I say to you who are hesitating about denying or confessing: acknowledge that ye have the Lord, lest, denying Him, ye be delivered up to prison. If the heathen chastise their slaves, when one of them denies his master, what, think ye, will your Lord do, who has authority over all men? Put away these counsels out of your hearts, that you may live continually unto God."

CHAPTER XXIX

"And they who believed from the twelfth mountain, which was white, are the following: they are as infant children, in whose hearts no evil originates; nor did they know what wickedness is, but always remained as children. Such accordingly, without doubt, dwell in the kingdom of God, because they defiled in nothing the commandments of God; but they remained like children all the days of their life in the same mind. All of you, then, who shall remain stedfast, and be as children, without doing evil, will be more honoured than all who have been previously mentioned; for all infants are honourable before God, and are the first persons with Him. Blessed, then, are ye who put away wickedness from yourselves, and put on innocence. As the first of all will you live unto God."

After he had finished the similitudes of the mountains, I said to him, "Sir, explain to me now about the stones that were taken out of the plain, and put into the building instead of the stones that were taken out of the tower; and about the round stones that were put into the building; and those that still remain round."

CHAPTER XXX

"Hear," he answered, "about all these also. The stones taken out of the plain and put into the building of the tower instead of those that were rejected, are the roots of this white mountain. When, therefore, they who believed from the white mountain were all found guileless, the Lord of the tower commanded those from the roots of this mountain to be cast into the building of the tower; for he knew that if these stones were to go to the building of the tower, they would remain bright, and not one of them become black. But if he had so resolved with respect to the other mountains, it would have been necessary for him to visit that tower again, and to cleanse it. Now all these persons were found white who believed, and who will yet believe, for they are of the same race. This is a happy race, because it is innocent. Hear now, further, about these round and shining stones. All these also are from the white mountain. Hear, moreover, why they were found round: because their riches had obscured and darkened them a little from the truth, although they never departed from God; nor did any evil word proceed out of their mouth, but all justice, virtue, and truth. When the Lord, therefore, saw the mind of these persons, that they were born good, and could be good, He ordered their riches to be cut down, not to be taken away for ever, that they might be able to do some good with what was left them; and they will live unto God, because they are of a good race. Therefore were they rounded a little by the chisel, and put in the building of the tower.

CHAPTER XXXI

"But the other round stones, which had not yet been adapted to the building of the tower, and had not yet received the seal, were for this reason put back into their place, because they are exceedingly round. Now this age must be cut down in these things, and in the vanities of their riches, and then they will meet in the kingdom of God; for they must of necessity enter into the kingdom of God, because the Lord has blessed this innocent race. Of this race, therefore, no one will perish; for although any of them be tempted by the most wicked devil, and commit sin, he will quickly return to his Lord. I deem you happy, I, who am the messenger of repentance, whoever of you are innocent as children, because your part is good, and honourable before God. Moreover, I say to you all, who have received the seal of the Son of God, be clothed with simplicity, and be not mindful of offences, nor remain in wickedness. Lay aside, therefore, the recollection of your offences and bitternesses, and you will be formed in one spirit. And heal and take away from you those wicked schisms, that if the Lord of the flocks come, He may rejoice concerning you. And He will rejoice, if He find all things sound, and none of you shall perish. But if He find any one of these sheep strayed, woe to the shepherds! And if the shepherds themselves have strayed, what answer will they give Him for their flocks? Will they perchance say that they were harassed by their flocks? They will not be believed, for the thing is incredible that a shepherd could suffer from his flock; rather will he be punished on account of his falsehood. And I myself am a shepherd, and I am under a most stringent necessity of rendering an account of you.

CHAPTER XXXII

"Heal yourselves, therefore, while the tower is still building. The Lord dwells in men that love peace, because He loved peace; but from the contentious and the utterly wicked He is far distant. Restore to Him, therefore, a spirit sound as ye received it. For when you have given to a fuller a new garment, and desire to receive it back entire at the end, if, then, the fuller return you a torn garment, will you take it from him, and not rather be angry, and abuse him, saying, 'I gave you a garment that was entire: why have you rent it, and made it useless, so that it can be of no use on account of the rent which you have made in it?' Would you not say all this to the fuller about the rent which you found in your garment? If, therefore, you grieve about your garment, and complain because you have not received it entire, what do you think the Lord will do to you, who gave you a sound spirit, which you have rendered altogether useless, so that it can be of no service to its possessor? for its use began to be unprofitable, seeing it was corrupted by you. Will not the Lord, therefore, because of this conduct of yours regarding His Spirit, act in the same way, and deliver you over to death? Assuredly, I say, he will do the same to all those whom He shall find retaining a recollection of offences. Do not trample His mercy under foot, He says, but rather honour Him, because He is so patient with your sins, and is not as ye are. Repent, for it is useful to you."

CHAPTER XXXIII

"All these things which are written above, I, the Shepherd, the messenger of repentance, have showed and spoken to the servants of God. If therefore ye believe, and listen to my words, and walk in them, and amend your ways, you shall have it in your power to live: but if you remain in wickedness, and in the recollection of offences, no sinner of that class will live unto God. All these words which I had to say have been spoken unto you."

The Shepherd said to me, "Have you asked me everything?" And I replied, "Yes, sir." "Why did you not ask me about the shape of the stones that were put into the building, that I might explain to you why we filled up the shapes?" And I said, "I forgot, sir." "Hear now, then," he said, "about this also. These are they who have now heard my commandments, and repented with their whole hearts. And when the Lord saw that their repentance was good and pure, and that they were able to remain in it, He ordered their former sins to be blotted out. For these shapes were their sins, and they were levelled down, that they might not appear."

Similitude Tenth

Concerning Repentance and Alms-Giving

CHAPTER I

After I had fully written down this book, that messenger who had delivered me to the Shepherd came into the house in which I was, and sat down upon a couch, and the Shepherd stood on his right hand. He then called me, and spoke to me as follows: "I have delivered you and your house to the Shepherd, that you may be protected by him." "Yes, sir," I said. "If you wish, therefore, to be protected," he said, "from all annoyance, and from all harsh treatment, and to have success in every good work and word, and to possess all the virtues of righteousness, walk in these commandments which he has given you, and you will be able to subdue all wickedness. For if you keep those commandments, every desire and pleasure of the world will be subject to you, and success will attend you in every good work. Take unto yourself his experience and moderation, and say to all that he is in great honour and dignity with God, and that he is a president with great power, and mighty in his office. To him alone throughout the whole world is the power of repentance assigned. Does he seem to you to be powerful? But you despise his experience, and the moderation which he exercises towards you."

CHAPTER II

I said to him, "Ask himself, sir, whether from the time that he has entered my house I have done anything improper, or have offended him in any respect." He answered, "I also know that you neither have done nor will do anything improper, and therefore I speak these words to you, that you may persevere. For he had a good report of you to me, and you will say these words to others, that they also who have either repented or will still repent may entertain the same feelings with you, and he may report well of these to me, and I to the Lord." And I said, "Sir, I make known to every man the great works of God: and I hope that all those who love them, and have sinned before, on hearing these words, may repent, and receive life again." "Continue, therefore, in this ministry, and finish it. And all who follow out his commands shall have life, and great honour with the Lord. But those who do not keep his commandments, flee from his life, and despise him. But he has his own honour with the Lord. All, therefore, who shall despise him, and not follow his commands, deliver themselves to death, and every one of them will be guilty of his own blood. But I enjoin you, that you obey his commands, and you will have a cure for your former sins."

CHAPTER III

"Moreover, I sent you these virgins, that they may dwell with you. For I saw that they were courteous to you. You will therefore have them as assistants, that you may be the better able to keep his commands: for it is impossible that these commandments can be observed without these virgins. I see, moreover, that they abide with you willingly; but I will also instruct them not to depart at all from your house: do you only keep your house pure, as they will delight to dwell in a pure abode. For they are pure, and chaste, and industrious, and have all influence with the Lord. Therefore, if they find your house to be pure, they will remain with you; but if any defilement, even a little, befall it, they will immediately withdraw from your house. For these virgins do not at all like any defilement." I said to him, "I hope, sir, that I will please them, so that they may always be willing to inhabit my house. And as he to whom you entrusted me has no complaint against me, so neither will they have." He said to the Shepherd, "I see that the servant of God wishes to live, and to keep these commandments, and will place these virgins in a pure habitation." When he had spoken these words he again delivered me to the Shepherd, and called those virgins, and said to them, "Since I see that you are willing to dwell in his house, I commend him and his house to you, asking that you withdraw not at all from it." And the virgins heard these words with pleasure.

CHAPTER IV

The angel then said to me, "Conduct yourself manfully in this service, and make known to every one the great things of God, and you will have favour in this ministry. Whoever, therefore, shall walk in these commandments, shall have life, and will be happy in his life; but whosoever shall neglect them shall not have life, and will be unhappy in this life. Enjoin all, who are able to act rightly, not to cease well-doing; for, to practice good works is useful to them. And I say that every man ought to be saved from inconveniences. For both he who is in want, and he who suffers inconveniences in his daily life, is in great torture and necessity. Whoever, therefore, rescues a soul of this kind from necessity, will gain for himself great joy. For he who is harassed by inconveniences of this kind, suffers equal torture with him who is in chains. Moreover many, on account of calamities of this sort, when they could not endure them, hasten their own deaths. Whoever, then, knows a calamity of this kind afflicting a man, and does not save him, commits a great sin, and becomes guilty of his blood. Do good works, therefore, ye who have received good from the Lord; lest, while ye delay to do them, the building of the tower be finished, and you be rejected from the edifice: there is now no other tower a-building. For on your account was the work of building suspended. Unless, then, you make haste to do rightly, the tower will be completed, and you will be excluded."

After he had spoken with me he rose up from the couch, and taking the Shepherd and the virgins, he departed. But he said to me that he would send back the Shepherd and the virgins to my dwelling. Amen.

Elucidations

I

The reader has now had an opportunity of judging for himself whether the internal evidence favours any other view of the authorship of The Shepherd, than that which I have adopted. Its apparent design is to meet the rising pestilence of Montanism, and the perils of a secondary stage of Christianity. This it attempts to do by an imaginary voice from the first period. Avoiding controversy, Hermas presents, in the name of his earlier synonyme, a portraiture of the morals and practical godliness which were recognised as "the way of holiness" in the apostolic days. In so doing, he falls into anachronisms, of course, as poets and romancers must. These are sufficiently numerous to reveal the nature of his production, and to prove that the author was not the Hermas of the story.

The authorship was a puzzle and a problem during the earlier discussions of the learned. An anonymous poem (falsely ascribed to Tertullian, but very ancient) did, indeed, give a clue to the solution:—

"—deinde Pius, Hermas cui germine frater,
Angelicus Pastor, quia tradita verba locutus."

To say that there was no evidence to sustain this, is to grant that it doubles the evidence when sufficient support for it is discovered. This was supplied by the fragment found in Milan, by the erudite and indefatigable Muratori, about a hundred and fifty years ago. Its history, with very valuable notes on the fragment itself, which is given entire, may be found in Routh's Reliquiæ. Or the English reader may consult Westcott's very luminous statement of the case. I am sorry that Dr. Donaldson doubts and objects; but he would not deny that experts, at least his equals, accept the Muratorian Canon, which carries with it the historic testimony needed in the case of Hermas. All difficulties disappear in the light of this evidence. Hermas was brother of Pius, ninth Bishop of Rome (after Hyginus, circ. a.d. 157), and wrote his prose idyl under the fiction of his Pauline predecessor's name and age. This accounts (1) for the existence of the work, (2) for its form of allegory and prophesying, (3) for its anachronisms, (4) for its great currency, and (5) for its circulation among the Easterns, which was greater than it enjoyed in the West; and also (6) for their innocent mistake in ascribing it to the elder Hermas.

1. The Phrygian enthusiasm, like the convulsionism of Paris in the last century, was a phenomenon not to be trifled with; especially when it began to threaten the West. This work was produced to meet so great an emergency.

2. "Fire fights fire," and prophesyings are best met by prophesyings. These were rare among the Orthodox, but Hermas undertook to restore those of the apostolic age; and I think this is what is meant by the tradita verba of the old poem, i.e., words "transmitted or bequeathed traditionally" from the times of Clement. Irenæus, the contemporary of this Hermas, had received the traditions of the same age from Polycarp: hence the greater probability of my conjecture that the brother of Pius compiled many traditional prophesyings of the first age.

3. Supposing the work to be in fact what it is represented to be in fiction, we have seen that it abounds with anachronisms. As now explained, we can account for them: the second Hermas forgets himself, like other poets, and mixes up his own period with that which he endeavours to portray.

4 and 5. Written in Greek, its circulation in the West was necessarily limited; but, as the plague of Montanism was raging in the East, its Greek was a godsend, and enabled the Easterns to introduce it everywhere as a useful book. Origen values it as such; and, taking it without thought to be the work of the Pauline Hermas, attributes to it, as a fancy of his own, that kind of inspiration which pertained to early "prophesyings." This conjecture once started, "it satisfied curiosity," says Westcott, "and supplied the place of more certain information; but, though it found acceptance, it acquired no new strength."

6. Eusebius and Jerome merely repeat the report as an on dit, and on this slender authority it travelled down. The Pauline Hermas was credited with it; and the critics, in their researches, find multiplied traces of the one mistake, as did the traveller whose circuits became a beaten road under the hoofs of his own horse.

If the reader will now turn back to the Introductory Note of the Edinburgh editors, he will find that the three views of which they take any serious notice are harmonized by that we have reached. (1) The work is unquestionably, on its face, the work of the Pauline Hermas. (2) But this is attributable to the fact that it is a fiction, or prose poem. (3) And hence it must be credited to the later Hermas, whose name and authorship are alone supported by external testimony, as well as internal evidence.

II

(Similitude Ninth, cap. xi. p. 47, note 1.)

Westcott is undoubtedly correct in connecting this strange passage with one of the least defensible experiments of early Christian living. Gibbon finds in this experiment nothing but an opportunity for his scurrility. A true philosopher will regard it very differently; and here, once and for all, we may speak of it somewhat at length. The young believer, a member, perhaps, of a heathen family, daily mixed up with abominable manners, forced to meet everywhere, by day, the lascivious hetæræ of the Greeks or those who are painted by Martial among the Latins, had no refuge but in flying to the desert, or practising the most heroic self-restraint if he remained with the relations and companions of his youth. If he went to the bath, it was to see naked women wallowing with vile men: if he slept upon the housetop, it was to throw down his mat or rug in a promiscuous stye of men and women. This alike with rich and poor; but the latter were those among whom the Gospel found its more numerous recruits, and it was just these who were least able to protect themselves from pollutions. Their only resource was in that self-mastery, out of which sprung the Encraty of Tatian and the Montanism of Tertullian. Angelic purity was supposed to be attainable in this life; and the experiment was doubtless attended with some success, among the more resolute in fastings and prayer. Inevitably, however, what was "begun in the spirit," ended "in the flesh," in many instances. To live as brothers and sisters in the family of Christ, was a daring experiment; especially in such a social atmosphere, and amid the domestic habits of the heathen. Scandals ensued. Canonical censures were made stringent by the Church; and, while the vices of men and the peril of persecution multiplied the anchorites of the desert, this mischief was crushed out, and made impossible for Christians. "The sun-clad power of chastity," which Hermas means to depict, was no doubt gloriously exemplified among holy men and women, in those heroic ages. The power of the Holy Ghost demonstrated, in many instances, how true it is, that, "to the pure, all things are pure." But the Gospel proscribes everything like presumption and "leading into temptation." The Church, in dealing with social evils, often encouraged a recourse to monasticism, in its pure form; but this also tended to corruption. To charge Christianity, however, with rash experiments of living which it never tolerated, is neither just nor philosophical. We have in it an example of the struggles of individuals out of heathenism,—by no means an institution of Christianity itself. It was a struggle, which, in its spirit, demands sympathy and respect. The Gospel has taught us to nauseate what even a regenerated heathen conceived to be praiseworthy, until the Christian family had become a developed product of the Church.

The Gospel arms its enemies against itself, by elevating them infinitely above what they would have been without its influences. Refined by its social atmosphere, but refusing its sanctifying power, they gloat over the failures and falls of those with whom their own emancipation was begun. Let us rather admire those whom she lifted out of an abyss of moral degradation, but whose struggles to reach the high levels of her precepts were not always successful. Yet these very struggles were heroic; for all their original habits, and all their surroundings, were of the sort "which hardens all within, and petrifies the feeling."

The American editor has devoted more than his usual amount of annotation to Hermas, and he affectionately asks the student not to overlook the notes, in which he has condensed rather than amplified exposition. It has been a labour of love to contribute something to a just conception of The Shepherd, because the Primitive Age has often been reproached with its good repute in the early churches. So little does one generation comprehend another! When Christians conscientiously rejected the books of the heathen, and had as yet none of their own, save the Sacred Scriptures, or such scanty portions of the New Testament as were the treasures of the churches, is it wonderful that the first effort at Christian allegory was welcomed, especially in a time of need and perilous temptation?

Printed in Great Britain
by Amazon

42905769R00109